Getting Published in Academic Journals

NAVIGATING THE PUBLICATION PROCESS

Brian Paltridge

University of Sydney

AND

Sue Starfield

UNSW Australia

Ann Arbor

Unversity of Michigan

ISBN-13: 978-0-472-03540-3 (paper)
ISBN-13: 978-0-472-12298-1 (ebook)

2019   2018   2017   2016   4   3   2   1

Acknowledgments

We thank the students who have taken part in our writing for publication courses and the people who have attended our presentations on this topic for the feedback they have given us on the material contained in this book. We also thank the reviewers of draft chapters for their detailed and helpful feedback on what we have written as well as those colleagues who have allowed us to share examples from reviews they have received. Our thanks as well to Kelly Sippell for her support and advice in the development of this book. We also thank John Swales and Christine Feak for their feedback on earlier drafts of the book, material they have provided for the book and, more broadly, the support they have shown for our work. And we are, as always, thankful to our families and life partners for their support and forbearance as we pursue our various academic endeavors.

Brian Paltridge
Sue Starfield

Contents

Introduction

This guide to getting published in academic journals draws on our experience as successful published authors, as teachers of courses in writing for publication, as reviewers of articles for academic journals, and as editors of peer-reviewed journals. We have also published research on scholarly publication more broadly.

Getting Published in Academic Journals is aimed, in particular, at graduate students and newly graduated PhDs who are wanting to but have not yet had their research published in peer-reviewed academic journals. It aims to help you gain an understanding of what you need to know and be able to do in order to get your work published in scholarly journals.

The book is written to be used in classes and workshops, especially as a supplement to the books in the revised and updated *English in Today's Research World* series (published by the University of Michigan Press). It can also be used as a stand-alone text for academic writers working by themselves.

Because we are passing on our experience in getting published, we have elected to tell some stories and refer to ourselves by our first names in the text.

═ Orientation ═

One highly regarded author had this to say about writing for publication: "As an academic more and more you live by virtue of your writing . . . if you don't join that race, you might lose opportunities professionally and so on" (Carnell et al., 2008, p. 45). We completely agree with this point, especially when it comes to graduate students and newly graduated PhDs. You need people to get to know your work, beyond the institutional context of your dissertation, as early on as possible. This is crucial in today's world where there is increasingly more competition for the academic and/or professional opportunities you are hoping your doctoral work will lead you to (see Chapter 2 for further discussion of this).

Writing for publication is a way in which people get to know you, and your work, before they meet you and, many times, instead of meeting you. Brian had exactly this experience when he submitted his first peer-reviewed article to an academic journal (Paltridge, 1992) before he had completed his doctoral studies. The editors of the journal at the time have since become strong supporters of his work even though he did not physically meet them until a good number of years after he had submitted that very first article to their journal. They have since gone on to be reviewers of his work for other publishers and have been referees for job and promotion applications. Of course, he didn't imagine this would happen when he sent his paper to their journal, but that first step in "joining the race" became an extremely important one for him, even though he didn't realize it at the time.

═ Why Write for Publication? ═

There are many reasons why you would want to write for publication. In her book *How to Get Research Published in Journals*, Abby Day (2007) lists some of these. The first of these is *clarity*; that is, the act of writing helps you to clarify your thinking about what you are doing. Writing also forces you to *revisit your ideas* and *re-examine* what you have done. It is also an opportunity for you to get *feedback* on your work, both from colleagues on drafts of your writing and then from reviewers once you have sent your article to a journal for consideration.

Getting published in academic journals also provides *tangible evidence* of your capability in your particular field. It *enhances your reputation* in the field, especially if you publish in international peer-reviewed journals. Publishing also puts you in contact with other people in your field. You may never meet some of these people face to face, but through your publishing, key people will get to know you and your work.

Publishing in academic journals, then, provides a *wider readership* for your work. It is an important way in which you can inform other people about your work, as well as influence other academics and the field more generally. It is not always (or even often) the case that a doctoral dissertation will do this. In fact, far fewer people read a PhD dissertation than many students imagine.

In a review one of us conducted of doctoral research a few years back, we found it surprisingly difficult to get copies of the dissertations we wanted to read. Some were available online through the university library, but many were not. Some could not be borrowed, so we had to purchase them in order to read them. The message to new academic writers, then, is if you want people to know about your work, you need to publish it!

Academic institutions all over the world are increasingly being held responsible for their research output, and the number of publications by their faculty is one way that this can be measured. Academic institutions also use publications as part of their appointment and promotion processes as they provide evidence of a person's ability to succeed in this area of academic life.

Getting published in academic journals, importantly, *adds to the body of knowledge* that is part of your field of study. A field only grows because people add to it. Getting published is how you are able to let people know about your research, your findings, and your ideas. It is where you can start to become part of the professional conversation of your discipline. As Rocco (2011) argues, a lot of new knowledge can be lost because new writers often do not know how to "join the conversation" in their disciplinary community. Your writing and the ability to get it published shows that you are able to do this.

In some countries, such as Iran, China, and the Netherlands, it is a requirement that parts of a doctoral dissertation have already been published in order for a student to graduate. The PhD regulations at the University of Amsterdam, for example, say that the dissertation "is a single academic treatment of a particular subject or a number of separate academic treatments, some or all of which have already been published, which together provide a cohesive study of a particular subject" (Universiteit van Amsterdam, 2010, p. 20). This kind of policy is clearly a factor in the increase, in recent years, of submissions of papers from writers in non-Anglophone countries to international peer-reviewed journals.

In some disciplines, the practice is to write a dissertation that is based on a compilation of publishable (and sometimes published) research articles, sometimes referred to as a *"PhD by publication."* These PhDs are quite different from other sorts of dissertations in that the research article chapters are more concise than typical dissertations chapters, making them more easily submitted to academic journals as stand-alone pieces of work.

The pressure on graduate students and newly graduated PhDs to publish their work continues to grow. Once, it was enough to have a PhD to secure an academic appointment. Those days are gone, and today academic institutions typically look for a strong *research trajectory* when making academic appointments. A typical question an appointment committee member might ask when looking at a job

One of us has a friend who decided to do a PhD by publication. She had been an academic for some years (without a PhD) and had many publications, but had found that she needed the PhD to move to other jobs in her field. She didn't want, however, to stop publishing while she did the PhD because this would create a gap in her publications resume. So she decided to do her PhD by publication. She was, thus, able to maintain her publishing profile at the same time as gaining her doctorate. And, she went on to get the job she was after, and at a much more senior level than she would have otherwise been considered for.

application is: "Does this candidate have a five-year coherent research agenda?" Having your work published in academic journals is a way in which you can demonstrate an agenda. Equally, newly appointed faculty members who are in tenure-track positions face the "publish or perish" dictate, particularly in the first years of their academic appointment. Simply put, writing and publishing are a measure of career success within the academy.

There is, however, more involved in the process of getting published in academic journals than new authors imagine. It is not simply a case of sending a coursework assignment to a journal or taking a PhD dissertation apart and sending sections of it to different journals.

There is much more to this process than writers who are new to getting published realize, especially when negotiating the submission and review process that is key to successful publication. The aim of this book is to clarify some of these issues and to offer advice—based on our experiences of getting our own work published, reviewing the work of others, editing academic journals, and drawing on our research into the structure of journal articles—to help you navigate this important academic rite of passage. As has been said, writing is "a means of saying who you are, locating yourself in the world, and representing yourself in the world" (Carnell et al., 2008, p. 9). This book will help you do that.

As journal editors we have always been able to spot an article that has been taken from a dissertation without being revised for the new and different audience. Sometimes it as simple as the author saying, "This chapter discusses … ." Other times we can see from an out-of-date reference list that the article is based on a dissertation that was submitted several years earlier and the author is only now starting to publish his or her work without having updated the research on which it is based. In both of these cases the author might have the article rejected without review. Our advice is to publish from your dissertation as soon as you can, considering the new and different audience for your article as you do this (a matter we return to in Chapter 1).

Chapter 1

Writing for Academic Journals

Writing for publication is never an easy task, whether for new or established writers. Nicola Johnson (2011) describes this process as "negotiating a crowded jungle." As she argues, a jungle is always crowded, which means that navigating the jungle can be difficult, even for people who have experience. Navigating a jungle is like entering unmarked territory, about which, especially for a beginning writer, much is unknown (Johnson, 2011). Because being in a jungle can be an exhilarating and rewarding experience, she argues that it's important to persist and not be knocked off track by what may seem to be insurmountable obstacles that can, in fact, be overcome (Johnson, 2011). Hyland (2015) also points out that although getting published in academic journals may seem to be a daunting task, it is not impossible. After all, millions of scholars do it every year, and so can you.

Understanding what, in your institution's eyes and your academic world more generally, is an acceptable research publication and the ethical standards you are expected to follow when writing for publication is essential. You also need to be able to write for an academic audience and in a style that is appropriate for that audience. It is also important to be able to make time for your writing and to find ways to get feedback on your writing so that it is as good as it can be before you submit it to a journal.

If you are a graduate student, you may be able to revise and then publish some of the papers you wrote in the coursework component of your degree. This, however, is not as easy as many people think as the work that has gone into a coursework assignment is usually not at the level of depth and detail that is required for a peer-reviewed journal article, no matter how high a grade the assignment was awarded. Or, if you are in the final stages of your doctorate, you may be able to break up your dissertation into smaller, stand-alone publishable size pieces, a topic that is discussed later in this chapter (see pages 14–15).

What Is an Acceptable Research Publication?

Institutions (and sometimes governments) have particular expectations for journal articles for them to be considered "acceptable" for hiring and promotion. The first expectation is that the article represents the *creation of new knowledge* or represents existing knowledge that has been used in a new and creative way such that it generates new concepts, methodologies, and understandings that lead to new understandings about the topic and, therefore, the creation of new knowledge (Department of Industry, Innovation, Science, Research and Tertiary Education, 2012). The research may also be acceptable if it includes the analysis of previous research, such as is the case with meta-analyses or what are sometimes termed *research syntheses* (Ortega, 2015).

Acceptable research publications for hiring and promotion are typically books, book chapters, journal articles, and (in some disciplines) refereed conference proceedings. Each article or chapter needs to show evidence of scholarly activity, be situated in the relevant literature on the topic, and be presented in such a way that allows readers to trace sources of the work being discussed, for example, through relevant citations and sometimes footnotes. The work also needs to be original and to have been through a journal or publisher's peer review process.

The article you write also needs to add to what we know about the topic by making a comparison between what the study you report on revealed and what is already known about the topic; that is, the piece of research needs to move the field forward in some way (see Chapter 3 for further discussion of this).

Students are often attracted to the idea of carrying out a meta-analysis because they do not have to collect new data. Conducting this kind of research, however, is not as easy as many people think. The first challenge is to find **all** of the research on the topic and to then compare the research that, very often, has been carried out in different ways, in different contexts, and with data sets that are not in fact comparable. One of us had this experience when we received funding from a major research institution to carry out research on a topic about which the institution was very keen to have a definitive answer. The research we found was difficult to compare, and the results of what comparisons we were able to make were extremely inconclusive. Had we not been funded for the project, we would have dropped it once we realised this problem, but because we had already received much of the funding we were, of course, obliged to continue with it. So what started off as a very good idea ended up being very hard work and something we would have given up on, had we been able to.

A student recently asked about the kinds of publications he should aim for while doing his doctorate and how a hiring committee would view these publications. Specifically, he asked about book reviews and conference proceedings as opposed to book chapters and journal articles. While writing book reviews will give you good experiences writing for publication and getting feedback on your writing from a journal's book review editor, they do not count as research. The standing of conference proceedings differs across disciplines but, for a conference proceedings publication to count as research, it needs to report on original research (it cannot, for example, be just a literature review) and your paper needs to have been peer reviewed. In addition, it needs to be a full article, not just the abstract of your talk. Generally, books, book chapters, and journal articles carry the greatest weight; in some disciplines, journal articles are more highly regarded than book chapters. Some universities, like Sue's, now list what they term "quality" journals and publishers and where they would like their faculty to publish. Some governments also have similar lists of rankings. It is worth finding out whether there is a policy you should be aware of when deciding where to send your work for publication.

Ethical Issues in Writing for Publication

In a position statement on responsible research publication for authors developed at the Second World Conference on Research Integrity, Wager and Kleinert (2011), the Chair and Vice-Chair of the Committee on Publication Ethics (COPE) (http://publicationethics.org) at the time, list a number of ethical issues relevant to researching and writing for publication. The following list summarizes the points they make:

- ❑ The research being reported should have been conducted in an ethical and responsible manner and should comply with all relevant legislation.

- ❑ Researchers should present their results clearly, honestly, and without fabrication, falsification, or inappropriate data manipulation.

- ❑ Researchers should strive to describe their methods clearly and unambiguously so that their findings can be confirmed by others.

- ❑ Researchers should adhere to publication requirements that submitted work is original, is not plagiarized, and has not been published elsewhere.

- ❑ Authors should take collective responsibility for submitted and published work.

- ❑ The authorship of research publications should accurately reflect individuals' contributions to the work and its reporting.

- ❑ Funding sources and relevant conflicts of interest should be disclosed.

This list indicates the importance of having followed your institutional review board's (or ethics committee's) requirements for conducting research and having permission to collect and use the data you included in your article in the way that you have. In fact, many journals now require authors to sign a statement to this effect before considering articles for publication.

Your research methods should also be described in detail, unless, of course, it is generally understood how you would do this in the field you are working in. You should also give detailed information about any participants involved in the study, the selection process, the instruments that were used, and the data collection and analysis procedures.

If yours is a qualitative study, you should show at least some of the data you are basing your interpretation on or at least make this data available to readers so that they can examine your data to confirm or reject the claim/s that you are making. To help you accomplish this, many journals now allow authors to submit supplementary material that will appear only in the online version (see Chapter 3 for further discussion on this).

The article you are writing, of course, needs to be original; none of the data used in the article should have been manipulated (or falsified) to suit your purpose and none of the article should be copied without appropriate acknowledgment from other sources. A blog titled *Retraction Watch* (retractionwatch.com/) lists cases of retracted journal articles with problems of this kind and gives explanations for the retractions.

The journal that Brian currently edits uses a program called *Ithenticate* (similar to *Turnitin®*) to check for plagiarism or, as it is sometimes called, *textual similarity*. Other journals use similar programs. Today, all articles are put through this type of program, and the editor is alerted if there are concerns about textual similarity. At that point, the editor has to make a judgment. Brian was once asked at a conference how much textual similarity is acceptable in a journal article. He was rather surprised by this question as the answer would typically be "none." The answer, however, is not as simple as this. Tables in the article that have been reproduced (with acknowledgement) from another source, for example, would still appear as textual similarity in the *Ithenticate* report but would not count as plagiarism. The same is true for the reference list and phrases such as *studies in second language acquisition have shown*. The user of the software can, however, exclude the reference list and phrases up to a certain length (say six words) from the report to get a better idea of the level of textual similarity. If, however, chunks of text have simply been copied word for word from other sources, then that would be a matter for concern. It can even be an issue if the copied text is from the author's own work, because this could indicate that the article or a very similar article has been published elsewhere, meaning that the recently submitted article is no longer an original submission. In this kind of situation, the author would get a message asking them to "please explain how your submission differs from the article you published on this topic in . . . ." If the author is not able to answer this question convincingly, it would lead, most likely, to a rejection.

Finally, any potential conflicts of interest in the article, such as a funding body that has an interest in the outcomes of the research, should be made clear in the article.

Expectations of Writing

Another aspect of writing a research article is knowing how to organize the article in a way that meets the expectations of a particular field of study and the field's journals. No one-size-fits-all way of writing research articles applies across all journals and disciplines, so it is important to get a sense of how you should write your article for the particular journal in which you would like it to be published.

It is also necessary to understand what you should include in your article and what you should leave out. For example, a very common mistake with submissions to peer-reviewed journals is a misunderstanding of what to include in the Discussion section of the article. Many writers think this is where they should "discuss" their findings, but this is only partly true. In the Discussion section, writers are expected to discuss their findings in relation to the previous research on their topic so that readers can see how the study that is being reported on contributes to extending knowledge in the field (see Swales & Feak, 2012; also Chapter 3 of this book).

It is also important in a research article to select only references that are relevant to the topic of the article rather than to the broader field, as may be the case with a dissertation. If you are using tabular data, it needs to tell a clear story that is appropriate to the argument you are making rather than simply showing that you have collected results.

Becoming Part of the Community

Lave and Wenger (1991) use the notion of *legitimate peripheral participation* as a way of capturing how people who are new to particular activities move from being an apprentice and on the periphery of a community to being part of the community—that is, a legitimate member of the particular community. In the case of writing for publication, this often involves what Lillis and Curry (2010) call *literacy brokers*—such as friends, advisors, colleagues, editors, reviewers, or proofreaders—who provide advice to academic writers. This is a perfectly acceptable practice and something that many successful writers do. Many publishers also offer editorial services (at a price) to authors, which is also an acceptable strategy for improving your writing (for further discussion, see Chapter 4 of Lillis & Curry, 2010; Chapter 6 of Paltridge, Starfield, & Tardy, 2016).

Literacy brokers can be divided into two main groups: *primary* and *secondary* readers. Friends, advisors, colleagues, and proofreaders are examples of secondary readers. While they may give valuable help and advice, they do not make the final judgment as to the quality of the research or the writing. It is the journal editor and the reviewers that will judge and be the primary readers (at this stage) for the text. Newer scholars often find this confusing as the advice they get from their secondary readers may be different from what they get from their primary readers. In the end, however, it is the primary readers of the submission (the editor and the reviewers) who can either accept the writing as consistent with the conventions and expectations of the target disciplinary community, or not (Johns, 1990). It is their advice, in the end, that needs to be followed.

Writing in an Appropriate Style

Writing in an appropriate academic style for a research article is extremely important. Accessible writing, in the words of Christine Casanave (2009, p. 300), "does not pack a million ideas into one sentence . . . . Long sentences can be unpacked and rewritten as several sentences, connected if needed by appropriate connecting words and phrases." Academic writing, she argues, may express difficult ideas, but it does not have to be overly dense.

In a response to an entry on the Guardian (U.K.) Higher Education Network blog (Anyangwe, 2012), Stephen Curry, a Professor of Structural Biology at Imperial College London, wrote, "It's all too easy to find examples of bad—i.e., dull—scientific writing but I think it's a mistake to think that one can write simultaneously for one's peers and the wider public. They are very different audiences."

In *Writing Readable Research*, Beverly Lewin (2010) discusses choosing appropriate vocabulary and grammar for the particular context and communicative purpose of the writing. She gives the following example of an article by Kelly Griffin (2005) published in a lifestyle journal for people who are over the age of 50 to illustrate features that are typical of articles written for a wider audience (in this case, a magazine) that are rather different from research articles published in academic journals:

> *You're Wiser Now*
>
> You react faster when you're young. There's no getting round it. But when people over 50 notice that they've lost a bit of the snap-crackle speed, they frequently overlook the mental powers they've gained in the bargain.
>
> Indeed, studies have shown that older adults are better at solving problems, more flexible in their strategies, and better able to bounce back from a bad mood more quickly.
>
> Keep that in mind the next time you're wandering through a parking lot looking for your car. (pp. 51–52)

As Lewin (2010) points out, the way in which this article is written is very conversational. Equally, although the article cites research, it does not conform to typical expectations for a research article. No statement of purpose of the research and no data are provided that readers can use to make their own judgment as to the reliability or validity of the research. The article includes a personal suggestion (*Keep that in mind the next time you're wandering through a parking lot looking for your car*) that is unlikely to occur in a research article. In terms of language, the frequent use of contractions such as *you're*, *there's*, and *they've* is common. No technical vocabulary appears in the article, and many of the sentences, noun groups (e.g., *people over 50* and *mental powers*), and paragraphs are very short. Further, the way in which other research is referred to is different from a research article where the studies that demonstrate the claims would typically be supported by in-text citations. The title of the article is equally conversational, with use of the personal pronoun *you*, which also contributes to the conversational style of the article.

When someone first starts to write academic texts, often the writing is full of very long sentences with very complex relationships between sentence parts. One reason for this is that new writers may be writing the way they speak. Halliday (1989) calls this *grammatical intricacy*, which is the way in which the relationship between clauses in spoken discourse is often much more spread out, and with more complex relationships between them, than in writing. Better academic writing is usually made up of shorter sentences with simpler relationships between clauses. Also, long noun groups (such as *the impacts of global warming on terrestrial ecosystems*) are typical of academic writing. These long noun groups do, however, make a text very dense and more complex for readers to process. Halliday (1989) calls this *lexical* density—a higher ratio of content words (such as *impacts*, *global warming*, and *terrestrial ecosystems)* to grammatical or function words (such as *of* and *on*) within a clause. While written texts do typically have higher lexical density than spoken texts, the lower this density, the easier a text is to read.

We often give students two texts on the same topic to read and compare: one from a magazine and the other a research article in an academic journal. We ask them to compare each of the pieces of writing in terms of grammar and vocabulary as well as how attributions to experts are made in each of the pieces of writing. We find that students often point out that the research article has features that are not typically found in magazine or newspaper articles. These features include:

- ❑ longer noun groups (e.g., *phenological trends in peer-reviewed journals*)
- ❑ many noun qualifiers (e.g., the noun group *Many studies* qualified by *examining the impacts of global warming on terrestrial ecosystems*)
- ❑ many technical items
- ❑ longer paragraphs
- ❑ many in-text references
- ❑ the use of a figure to summarize the text
- ❑ high lexical density
- ❑ frequent use of nominalization (e.g., *combination* as a noun rather than *combine* as a verb)

Writing for Audience

There are, then, substantial differences between writing for a broad, non-specialist audience, such as newspaper and magazine articles that are aimed at a lay audience, and writing for a specialist expert audience, as is the case with journal articles. In each of these cases, the language, writing style, and use of specialized terms varies. Key for writing for different audiences is developing a sense of who the audience is and what the appropriate level and style of language is for the particular communication.

In their book *Academic Writing for Graduate Students*, Swales and Feak (2012) argue for the importance of audience in academic writing. As they point out, even before you begin to write, you need to consider the audience for your writing, which includes an understanding of the audience's expectations and prior knowledge, because these will impact the content of the writing.

As one of the faculty members in Carnell et al.'s (2008) book *Passion and Politics: Academics Reflect on Writing for Publication* said:

> You write for an audience, basically, and you have to know who the audience is when you start out and the type of writing that's appropriate. Learning to write for a specific audience is a sub-branch of learning to write at all. . . . I think the principle of addressing the audience is one that all writing has to address upfront. (p. 31)

Chapter 3 returns to this topic.

Making Time for Your Writing

It is important to develop good organizational skills for managing your writing as well as making time to write. A faculty member at the University of London who was asked about this said that "you have to sit down and just organize your time, to ensure there are spaces for writing. To give it the priority it deserves" (Carnell et al., 2008, p. 25). This, of course, is not always as simple as it seems. Another faculty member at the same institution said:

> I think because I'm a mother . . . and because I've always worked full time, once the children were two or three, I had to multi-task when it came to writing. I have always had to work on trains, planes, at bus stations, [at] a doctor's surgery—anywhere where I could find ten or 15 minutes. The notion of sitting quietly down in a study endlessly writing for days just hasn't been my experience. (p. 26)

In a chapter in a book on writing for publication, Nackoney, Munn, and Fernandez (2011) say this about managing time for writing:

> In an ideal world, we would prefer to have large blocks of time to work on projects. However, this is not always possible. We therefore have to look for pockets of time

to write. . . . Sometimes the most opportune times are the easiest to overlook, such as using commuting time to write, read, take notes, and edit manuscripts. (p. 37)

It is important that you find the best way to do your writing. You might write anywhere and at any time you can do it. Or you might wait for large chunks of time to do the writing and only write when you have that time. If you do this, however, you may never find the time to write, or if you do, it may not be enough. The most productive approach, in Rowena Murray's (2013) view, is when people do both. Her research has shown that writing in short bursts can be extremely valuable and that many successful writers fit their writing into the time that is available to them rather than simply waiting to have "more time to write."

It is surprising, in fact, how much you can write in a short time. This is an exercise Murray asked the class to do at a recent workshop. The idea behind this task is to both generate text and the main ideas you would like to cover in your more extended piece of writing.

Think of an article you are presently working on and write a paragraph that summarizes the main theoretical and practical points you wish to make in the Conclusion section. Use the following prompts to help you do this:

❑ The main theoretical contribution of this article is … .

❑ The main practical contribution of this article is … .

Write without reference to any other material; just write what you have in mind that you want to say. Write for 5 minutes in full sentences without stopping. Let one other person read what you wrote (for example, a colleague or a fellow student), and ask him or her to give feedback on what you have written. Ask him or her to paraphrase what your main points are to make sure they are clear in your writing.

When Brian did this exercise, he was writing the Conclusions section for an article he had been working on with colleagues on the topic of doctoral writing in the visual and performing arts (Paltridge et al., 2012). This is what he wrote in the workshop on the practical contributions of the study:

> The main practical contribution of this article is in providing an understanding and the range of options that are available to visual and performing arts doctoral students for how they might organize their texts. The study, thus, provides insights into discourse practices in visual and performing arts doctoral writing and makes a contribution to genre studies and advanced academic literacies research more broadly. It has, further, demystified writing in in a way that is useful to both students and their supervisors. (p. 342)

This is how the text appeared, after revision and expansion, in the final published article, showing how valuable this kind of writing exercise is:

> From a practical point of view, our study has revealed that there is a range of options for how students might organize their texts in visual and performing arts doctorates but that they still need, in some way, to address the broader issues of what it is that characterizes successful doctoral writing. Notwithstanding this variation, the texts we examined are all examples of successful doctoral texts having all met the criteria set by universities for the examination of doctoral dissertations. Our study, then, offers insights into discourse practices in visual and performing arts doctoral writing as well as contributing to the broader areas of genre studies and advanced academic literacies research (Paltridge et al., 2012, p. 342).

Publishing from a Dissertation

Many PhD students look to produce research articles from their dissertation as the first step in disseminating their research. To do this, determine how you can derive smaller, sometimes bite-sized, pieces from your dissertation that will be suitable for research articles. If, for example, your study is made up of a number of case studies or separate experiments, these may be suitable for stand-alone articles. It may also be possible to create an article from preliminary work you did for your dissertation, such as a survey or a pilot study, that does not have a central place in your dissertation. Or you may have collected data that is not analyzed in detail in your dissertation but has the potential to be the basis for an article on its own.

Put simply, you should not see the process of getting articles from your dissertation as just a matter of cutting and pasting. You should also avoid what is sometimes called *salami publishing*—that is, dividing your dissertation into "the thinnest possible slices and submitting each slice as a separate article" (Kitchen & Fuller, 2005, p. 36) to a different journal or publishing the same work with only minor changes in different journals (see publicationethics.org/case/salami-publication for further discussion). You should also be aware that many publishers are now using similarity detection software to look for this in the same way that students are now, in some institutions, required to submit their written assignments to a program such as *Turnitin®* (turnitin.com/) before they submit their work.

It may also be that you wish to withhold your dissertation content until you are able to have parts of it published in academic journals. This practice is becoming increasingly common in the United States and in some other parts of the world because dissertations are often now publically available via digital repositories in university libraries once they have been accepted for the degree. There have also been cases where dissertations have been made available via the internet without the student's knowledge or permission. This could, perhaps, create problems when submitting parts of the dissertation for publication when it has already been "published" elsewhere.

New academic writers are often disconcerted, however, when they find they cannot seem to "get it right" the first time when writing for publication. What they do not realize is that published research articles have nearly always been through a number of drafts and multiple rewritings before they finally appear in print.

Converting a dissertation into research articles often requires substantial recontextualizing, reframing, reprioritizing, trimming, condensing, and even restructuring (Kwan, 2010). It is not usually as simple as taking a chapter from the dissertation and submitting it as an article. The research article needs to stand alone and be able to be read and valued by a much wider readership than that of the dissertation. Revising the dissertation for journal publication then "demands careful selecting and rewriting, as well as the difficult task of figuring out the most important points in the dissertation in order of importance" (Nonmore, 2011, pp. 85–86).

Brian produced five articles from his PhD. His dissertation was a comparative study of two different ways of analyzing research article Introductions. He published each of the analyses separately and then published an article which, in a much broader sense, compared the two. He also published an article (in the top ranking journal in his field) on an aspect of his analysis that he was sure his examiners would ask about (which, in fact, they didn't). He then published a more practical article for teachers, also in a high-ranking journal, that discussed how a key observation he made in his study could be taken up by language teachers. While all the journals he published in were highly regarded, he purposely chose the one aimed at language teachers as he was a language teacher himself and wanted to establish himself not only as a researcher in the field, but also as someone who knew what the implications of his work were for teachers. So he found stand-alone topics within the dissertation that he could publish in their own right, and that were not dependent on the larger piece of work in order to understand them.

Co-Authoring

Co-authoring is now becoming common in academic publishing. In 1988, for example, co-authoring represented only 8 percent of all published articles, but grew to 23 percent in 2009 (Ware & Mabe, 2015). Co-authoring is a strategy newer writers might want to consider—that is, writing and publishing with someone else, perhaps your advisor, or a senior graduate student. You may also wish to write with another student who is also a friend. Writing with a friend, however, does not guarantee success. Being friends and being able to work together are not the same thing. Regardless of with whom you write, each person should take responsibility for the article, and decisions to that effect should happen early in the process. It should not be left to just one person to do all the work.

Kitchin and Fuller (2005, p. 14) give this advice for working together on a publication:

- ❑ **Talk a lot:** Adopt a pattern of regular correspondence, swapping ideas and points of view.

- ❑ **Agree to disagree:** Do not expect to agree on every issue, keep disagreements in perspective, and be prepared to compromise.

- ❑ **Organize and plan:** Create roles for each person and make sure there is an agreed plan of action, with one person designated as the coordinator/moderator.

Regarding authorship, all authors who have made a substantial contribution to the work should be listed, and deserving authors should not be omitted (especially you). It is also important to clarify at the outset the order of names for the publication. In some areas of study, the key researcher's name will be first, but it will be last in other fields. It is important to learn how this works in your area of study and to discuss with your coauthor(s) where your name will appear in the final publication. This order is especially important as this is often something that job application and promotion committees consider (see Chapter 4 of Hyland, 2015, for further discussion of this).

Brian was once part of a promotions committee in a different department from the one in which he currently works. An applicant had many publications in which he was part of large team of authors, but his name was always listed in final position. What Brian discovered was that, in this particular field, this indicated that he was the most important author for the articles, whereas in Brian's field, it means the opposite. Therefore, it is important that this issue be clarified early so that you are not disappointed (or become resentful) if the names are not in the order you expect. Also, in some cases, an advisor's name is included in a student's publications, and in others it is not. This also seems to differ geographically. In Brian's case, none of the publications that he derived from his dissertation had his advisor's name on them, even though she had given him feedback on a number of them. A colleague of his who did her PhD at a European university in the same field, however, had the name of her advisor and those of the whole research team in which she was working included on all her publications, as this was clearly the local expectation.

Getting Feedback on Your Writing

Showing your writing to your peers is a very useful way of getting feedback on and improving your writing. It also prepares you for a key part of the writing for publication process and responding to reviewers' comments on your work. Pat Thomson's blog (2011) (patthomson.wordpress.com/2011/07/18/how-to-give-feedback-on-a-peers-paper/) gives advice to early-career writers on how to give and get feedback on their writing. Here are some of the points she makes:

- ❑ Be appreciative of what the other person wrote. The aim is not to tear strips off the piece but to encourage further writing. What you are reading is a draft and the writer is looking for helpful feedback, not an assassination.
- ❑ Remember to give feedback for improvement that is achievable.

She also suggests writers do these things as they review each others' work:

- ❑ Summarize the argument of the piece of writing so that the writer can see/hear whether you have grasped what they think they have said.

❑ Identify the contribution that you think the piece of writing makes. It might be helpful to think about what you know after you have read the writing that you didn't know before you read it.

❑ Identify the strengths of the piece of writing.

❑ Differentiate between secretarial tasks—spelling, grammar, paragraphs, headings, layout, forms of expression—and writing issues—whether the argument is clear, whether the question is addressed as promised, whether the writing is well organized and structured, and whether claims are justified given the evidence provided. (Thomson, 2011)

Figure 1.1 is a task Brian often uses with students in his writing for publication class.

The task shown in Figure 1.1 not only gives students other people's views on their writing, but it also gives them advice they can take to both improve and polish their writing. Brian usually asks students to do the task in groups of three or four. The students send each other the piece of writing they want feedback on several days before they meet so everyone has time to read and prepare feedback. The first time he did this he worried that it might not work and that students wouldn't be interested in reading each other's work. In fact, he found the opposite to be the case with one of the students saying as she left the room, "That was great! When can we do this again?"

Some of Brian's students have used the feedback task shown in Figure 1.1 as the starting point for forming their own writing groups. The students meet once a month and read and critique each other's writing in progress. They give each other suggestions on improving the content, as well as the quality, of the writing. It is a condition of coming to the meetings that everyone has read each other's work. If they haven't, there is a penalty—making a financial donation to a political party they didn't vote for!

=== **Figure 1.1** ===

Feedback Worksheet

Working with a peer, fellow writer, or writers' group participant, exchange an article or section of an article you have been working on. Use this worksheet to make notes on the piece of writing to provide feedback on what the other person wrote. When you have completed the worksheet, meet with each other to discuss your notes.

Title:	
Author:	
Summary of the argument:	
What I learned:	
Strengths:	
Clarity of the arguments:	
Organization and structure:	
Evidence provided to support claims:	
Suggestions for improvement:	
Reviewed by:	
Date:	

Writing Groups

Another way of improving your writing is to form a writing group with other students to give each other feedback on your writing. You can decide how big the group will be, how often it will meet, who should be members of the group, and what the focus of the group's meetings will be. The key thing, however, is that everyone should have an article they are working on for publication to take part in the group's meetings.

An advantage of forming writing groups is that it makes time for talking about writing as well as getting feedback on your writing. It also creates an opportunity for people to discuss their writing practices and to learn from what other people do. Writing groups provide an opportunity to share information about journals, editors, and reviewers, as well as to discuss reviewers' reports and how to deal with them. And, of course, writing groups can also be used to provide dedicated writing time where you can get together and just write. Writing groups, then, make time for writing, provide support for writing, and help develop productive writing strategies for the members of the group (Murray, 2013).

Writing boot camps are also becoming a popular way for beginning writers to have a period of uninterrupted time to focus on their work. These are often run for students who are working on a thesis or dissertation but can be just as useful for working on an academic article.

Chapter 2

Deciding Which Academic Journal to Publish In

The first thing to consider when preparing an article for publication is the journal to which to submit. There are several different kinds of academic journals and different factors that will affect your decision, each of which will be discussed in this chapter. Further, more journals are published now than at any time in the past. The International Association of Scientific, Technical and Medical Publishers reports that there were about 28,100 active publishers of academic journals in late 2014, among them about 2.5 million articles a year. Ninety-five percent of these publishers publish only one or two journals, whereas, at the other end of the scale, the five largest journal publishers—Elsevier, Sage, Springer, Taylor & Francis, and Wiley-Blackwell—publish nearly 35 percent of all journals (Ware & Mabe, 2015).

Many more authors are submitting their work to academic journals than ever in the past, and these numbers are still increasing, by about 3 percent per year (Hyland, 2015). While the United States represents about 23 percent of the global output of published research articles, there has been a dramatic growth in published research from China and East Asia. China, for example, now represents 17 percent of the global output of research articles, followed by the U.K. (7 percent), Japan (6 percent), Germany (6 percent), and France (4 percent) (Ware & Mabe, 2015). This means that the competition has increased for getting published in academic journals. It is especially important, then, that you understand the different kinds of journals that are being published and where you work might best fit. It is also important to have a sense of the standing of different academic journals, as this will also influence your decision as to where you will submit your article.

The Standing of Academic Journals

Impact Factors

Impact factors are one way in which you can get a sense of the standing of an academic journal. In her book *How to Get Research Published in Journals* (2007, pp. 73–74), Day says that the "impact factor is determined by measuring how often the 'average article' in any particular journal has been cited within a particular period (usually 2 years) and provides a ratio between citations and citable papers." (See www.hsl. virginia.edu/services/howdoi/hdi-jcr.cfm for information on how to find the impact factor for a journal.)

If a journal does not have an impact factor, it does not mean that you should not consider publishing in it. It takes some time before newer journals are eligible to be considered for an impact factor as they need to show their citation record as part of the impact factor application process. This is a problem for newer and slower-paced disciplines, so you should not use the impact factor as the sole driver for deciding where to submit an article.

We recently had the experience of sending an article to a highly regarded journal in our field, one in which leading figures publish. It turned out, however, not to have an impact factor, even though it was published by a leading journal publisher. It was still a good fit for our article because it crossed the two areas of our research—education and linguistics. People who are looking for research that covers these areas would no doubt look to this journal for articles such as ours and not be bothered, we would think, by whether it has an impact factor or not.

Impact factors, then, should be treated with caution. Impact factors are relative, and what may be considered high in one field may be considered low in another. The impact factor of a journal is not the same as the number of times an article has been hit or down-loaded, which may be a better indication of how the article has been accepted by practitioners (rather than researchers), how popular it is in more general terms, and how widely it has been disseminated. The first thing you should consider is your audience and your purpose. Review impact factors if you think more than one journal is suitable for your article.

Other Measures

One further metric that is now being used to show the standing of academic journals is the Immediacy Index (www.admin-apps. webofknowledge.com/JCR/help/h_immedindex.htm). This measure provides the average number of times articles are cited in a journal in the year in which they are published. It, thus, shows how quickly articles are cited in a particular journal following their publication. It is typically not as high as the journal's impact factor but is something you may want to look at as well.

Another metric is the Source Normalized Impact per Paper (SNIP) developed by Professor Henk Moed at the University of Leiden (http://www.journalmetrics.com/snip.php). The SNIP provides a citation impact by weighting a journal's citations against the total number of citations in a subject field. It provides a comparison between journals

An article Brian published some years ago (Paltridge, 2002) is still in the list of ten most downloaded articles on the journal's website even though it is not in the list of most cited articles in the journal. The article has also been republished (Paltridge, 2015b) in an edited collection that aims to bring together material that has been influential in the field based, not on how many times it has been cited, but on how many times it has been read. The level of downloading, thus, is another way of showing the impact of your work, other than citations.

as well as an indication of the probability of being cited when publishing in a particular journal.

The SCImago Journal & Country Rank web page (www.scimagojr.com/index.php) is also useful for getting a sense of the standing of different journals. The SCImago measure aims to provide a ranking of academic journals in terms of both the number of citations received by the journal and the importance or prestige of the journals where the citations were made. The SCImago website shows both the world and country ranking of journals and allows you to narrow your search to particular disciplinary areas and particular journal titles.

There are also metrics such as Almetrics (https://www.altmetric.com) which show how often and where work is cited on the internet. Clicking on an icon on the pages of an article reveals a record of where and how many times the work has been cited. These citations are from sources such as the mainstream media, public policy documents, blogs, Wikipedia and Twitter. Almetrics is used by Taylor & Francis, the University of Michigan Press, Duke University, the University of Manchester, and the University of Cambridge, for example, for their journals (see www.altmetric.com/case-studies/).

Acceptance Rates

Acceptance rates are another factor to consider when submitting an article to a journal. An acceptance rate is the percentage of articles that get published out of the total number of articles that were submitted to the journal in a given year. So if a journal has an acceptance rate of 10 percent, this means only 10 percent of the articles that were submitted to the journal over the year were finally accepted for publication. Thus, 90 percent of all articles that were submitted were rejected, meaning that the journal has a *rejection rate* of 90 percent. This information on acceptance rates can be difficult to find, but it is often needed for promotion and tenure applications where more prestige is given to journals with lower acceptance rates than those with higher ones. An acceptance rate of 10 percent or lower, thus, would be considered good by an appointments or promotion committee as it suggests it is difficult to get published in the journal. By contrast, an acceptance rate of 50 percent would not be considered good as it would suggest that it not difficult to get published in the journal and that the journal, concomitantly, is of lessor standing than one with a lower acceptance rate. The way in which the acceptance rate is calculated can differ among journals, however: Some journals use all manuscripts that were submitted in the year as the basis for calculating the rate, and others base the calculation on only the articles that were sent out for review. In these two cases, the former journal has a lower acceptance rate than the latter.

Sometimes the acceptance rate is in the Information for Authors or on the home page for the journal. If it is not there, you can email the editor for this information.

Types of Academic Journals

Peer-Reviewed Journals

Your preferred publishing outlet for your article will most probably be a peer-reviewed journal—that is, a journal where submissions have been reviewed by experts in the particular field (see Chapter 4 for a detailed discussion of peer review). There is a lot of competition when trying to get published in peer-reviewed journals, so you may have to balance your desire to get published with the likelihood of your work being accepted in a particular journal.

One strategy for deciding on a journal is to start at the top of your list of preferred journals (taking into account the kind of article you are writing and how good you believe it is) and to move down the list. Submit your article to the most prestigious journal where you think it will fit and, if it is rejected, move down the list from there. This is advice that Brian was given some years ago that he still finds helpful and considers when deciding where to submit an article. Do not, however, submit your article to more than one journal at the same time. This is not acceptable practice in academic publishing. Indeed, many journals will ask you to confirm—at the time that you are submitting your article—that it is not being considered for publication by any other journal at that time.

A journal's acceptance rate can be discouraging for new authors. These numbers do not, however, tell the full story. For example, the journal that Brian currently edits had an overall acceptance rate of 10.7 percent in 2014. This figure, however, is an average of a number of acceptance rates: 6.7 percent for full-length articles in regular issues, 6.3 percent for articles in a section titled Forum, 16.7 percent in a section titled Brief Reports and Summaries, 100 percent of Book Reviews, 23.1 percent in a section titled Research Issues, and 14.5 percent for full-length articles published in the annual special issue of the journal.

This tells you that you have more chance of getting published in the Brief Reports and Summaries section than you do with a regular full-length article in this journal. The Book Reviews figure looks encouraging, but these are always commissioned so it is not surprising that they were all accepted. The acceptance rate for full-length articles in special issues also looks encouraging. However, an initial screening process takes place for special issues where people are asked to send in a proposal and, on the basis of this, invited to submit a full article for consideration (or not). In 2014, the journal's special issue received 48 proposals of which 14.5 percent were finally accepted for publication. This is still a higher number than for articles in regular issues of the journal, so it does suggest that special issues are worth submitting to if they fit the focus of your article.

Other good news is that while Brian's journal rejected 57 percent of full-length article submissions without review in 2014, of those submissions that were sent for review, 64 percent were asked to make revisions to their article. Further, 75 percent of those authors who were asked to make revisions finally had their article accepted for publication. What this says is that if you are asked to revise your article, it is fairly likely it will be accepted for publication provided you revise your article as requested by the editor and reviewers.

Wendy Belcher (2009) breaks peer-reviewed journals into five categories, from the most prestigious to the least:

1. disciplinary journals
2. field journals
3. interdisciplinary journals
4. newer journals
5. regional journals

Each of these will be discussed.

Disciplinary Journals

Disciplinary journals publish scholarly peer-reviewed work in a specific discipline, such as Sociology, Anthropology, and Economics. Examples of disciplinary journals are the *American Sociological Review*, *American Anthropologist*, the *Journal of Economic Theory*, the *New England Journal of Medicine*, and the *Journal of Economic Perspectives*. Acceptance in these journals can be extremely difficult; they typically have a large number of submissions and often have a very low acceptance rate, often less than 10 percent. Disciplinary journals have a higher rejection rate than most field journals, and they are also broader in their scope than other types because they publish work that will appeal to a wider and more diverse audience.

Field Journals

While disciplinary journals have very high standing in their respective fields, you may have a better chance of getting your work published in a field journal. Field journals publish research in a subcategory of a discipline. Most academic journals are field journals. Examples of field journals are *Ophthalmology*, *Oral Microbiology and Immunology*, *Postcolonial Studies*, the *Harvard Review of African American Public Policy*, and *English for Specific Purposes*. Field journals typically have a higher acceptance rate than disciplinary journals. *English for*

Specific Purposes, for example, has an acceptance rate of about 14 percent whereas the related disciplinary journal, *Applied Linguistics*, has an acceptance rate of about 7 percent. Publishing in field journals helps frame your work in your area of specialization. These journals are still well regarded and will impress hiring and tenure committees because they show your standing and ability in the specific area in which you are working or want to work.

Interdisciplinary Journals

Interdisciplinary journals publish work that is informed by and spans more than one discipline. A journal might bring two disciplines together, as with *Philosophy and Public Affairs* and *Economy and Society*, or a journal may not fit neatly into one specific discipline, such as *Human Rights Quarterly*. Interdisciplinary journals are also well regarded and show your ability to work across fields and disciplines, which can also be a strength when applying for jobs or promotions.

Some years ago, Brian was invited to contribute to a special issue of the *IEEE Transactions on Professional Communication*, a journal that crosses the areas of professional communication, engineering, science, and business. The journal's website describes the readership of the journal as "technical communicators, engineers, scientists, information designers, editors, linguists, translators, managers, business professionals, and others from around the globe who practise, conduct research on, and teach others about effective professional communication" (IEEE, 2015), so it has a very wide readership. The article Brian wrote (Paltridge, 2000), titled "Genre knowledge and teaching professional communication," crossed the areas of technical communication, education, and linguistics by discussing a particular view of texts (genre) and outlining what this view had to offer the teaching of professional communication. His article, thus, showed his ability to work across disciplines as well as his understanding of how theoretical matters relate to practical applications.

Newer Journals

Newer journals—that is, journals that are three to seven years old—can be a good place for less experienced authors because they often have no backlog; that is, they do not have a set of accepted papers that are waiting to be assigned to the next issue of the journal. They are, thus, often in need of submissions. This increases your odds of getting published and of getting published sooner. Newer journals may also be more inclined to help new authors and allow numerous revisions to the article before accepting it for publication. More established journals, by contrast, may have a "two strikes and you're out" policy. In other words your article may be rejected if, after resubmission, it does not meet their acceptance criteria.

Regional Journals

Regional journals publish work from a particular area or location such as a particular country, region, province, or city. While regional journals may not be rated as highly as other journals, they may be a good starting point if your work falls within their focus. An example of a regional journal is the *Canadian Journal of Communication*, which describes its focus as:

> to publish Canadian research and scholarship in the field of communication studies. In pursuing this objective, particular attention is paid to research that has a distinctive Canadian flavor by virtue of choice of topic or by drawing on the legacy of Canadian theory and research. The purview of the journal is the entire field of communication studies as practiced in Canada or with relevance to Canada. (Canadian Journal of Communication, n.d.)

It is clear from this description that the work the journal publishes has to be about Canada. So, if your research is about Canada (and it's about communication), then this may be a good journal for you to consider for your article. If it is not about Canada, however, it less likely that the journal will be interested in your submission.

Publications That Are Not Peer Reviewed

Publications such as newspapers, magazines, and newsletters are not normally peer reviewed. Yet, publishing in these venues can add to your profile in the field. While they may not count in hiring and promotion processes as academic publications, they may demonstrate your engagement with a community or an issue and so might be favorably viewed in this sense.

Online Journals

Increased possibilities exist for publishing in online journals (only). Online journals are a way for your work to be published much more quickly and disseminated more widely than would be the case with print-based journals. A further advantage of these journals is that the numbers of hits on your article can be tracked, and it is easy for your work to be cited. Additionally, space is much less of a problem with online journals, which means that your article can be easily linked to externally stored data where it can be amplified and extended at no extra cost to the publisher. The move that most print-based journals have now made to having a mostly online presence (Ware & Mabe, 2012) has had the result of making the issue of space less of a priority for these journals. Perceptions about online-only journals are not always positive, however, and promotion and tenure committees do not always give equal weight to them as they do to journals that also have a print-based presence.

As is the case with any journal you select, be sure the online journal is peer reviewed, and has an editorial board made up of people who are working in your field. If the online publication has an institutional affiliation, it helps if it is one that is generally well regarded in your field. You should also look to see who contributes to the journal. For example, are the articles (or at least some of the articles) written by people who have standing in your field? Of course, not all of the contributions need be by the leaders in the field, but it helps if some of them are.

Unfortunately, some "predator" journals exist and take advantage of less experienced writers trying to get published. American Journal Experts (Prater, 2014) provides a list of indicators for considering whether a journal you are thinking about sending an article to is questionable. These indicators are:

- ❏ The journal asks for a submission fee (rather than a publication fee) that is payable whether or not the article is accepted.
- ❏ The editorial board is very small or listed as "coming soon."
- ❏ A single publisher releases a large number of new journals at the same time.
- ❏ The journal says an issue will be available at a certain time, but it never appears.
- ❏ The journal's website is not professional in quality.
- ❏ The journal's title suggests a national or international affiliation that does not match its editorial board or location.
- ❏ There are errors in article titles and their abstracts.
- ❏ The content of the journal varies from its title and stated scope.

Val Colic-Peisker (2012) reports the case of one of her students who submitted an article to an online journal. The article was accepted with no revisions only three weeks after the article had been submitted. This is very unusual as the review process normally takes about three months or more. The same message also asked for a $200 submission fee. Upon examination, Colic-Peisker found that someone else was using the name of the editor and that the student's letter had not come from the actual journal editor.

On his website (scholarlyoa.com/individual-journals/), Jeffery Beall (n.d.) provides a list of possible predatory journals. He also provides a list of publishers (scholarlyoa.com/publishers/) who may publish predatory journals. If you receive an email request for a submission to a journal that you have not had any contact with, it is worth

Predatory journals often say that the submissions they receive are peer reviewed but very often they are not, despite what they say on their websites. On a number of occasions, authors have submitted nonsense research articles to these journals just to test this out and have found the articles have been accepted with the claim that they went out for review when they very clearly did not. The articles, further, would have been published had the authors agreed to pay the publishing fee requested by the journal. Of course, they didn't pay the fee. They just wanted to see if articles that didn't make any sense would be accepted by one of these journals. And they were.

checking his list to see if the journal is listed. On another webpage (scholarlyoa.com/2012/11/30/criteria-for-determining-predatory-open-access-publishers-2nd-edition/), Beall provides further advice on how you can identify a predatory journal. He offers these clues:

❑ There is no academic information provided about the editor and members of the editorial board.

❑ The publisher's owner is named as the editor of the journal.

❑ The publisher does not reveal its physical location.

❑ The journal claims falsely to be listed in legitimate indexing services.

Open Access Journals

Some online journals may also be *open access* (OA), meaning that readers do not have to subscribe to the journal in order to obtain access to your article. The advantage here is that people can read and cite your work more easily than with other publishing models. Once again, the journal needs to be peer reviewed and have scholarly standards because this will influence the degree of esteem that your article will receive and how valuable it will be for your career.

Some governments, such as the U.K., have mandated open access for research articles that result from work that they have funded. A number of publishers are responding to this by delaying open access to their journals for a year after the initial date of publication; others delay the open access beyond that. If you want your article to be open immediately you may have to pay a fee. The pricing information for early open access is usually listed on the journal's homepage and can range from $500 to $5,000 (U.S. dollars).

An increasing number of journals are now being published by reputable publishers that are both online and open access, so you cannot necessarily assume, just because a journal is online and open access, that it is a questionable or predatory journal. The standing of the publisher is one way in which you can ascertain whether the journal is bona fide or not. Springer, for example, has recently launched a range of journals under SpringerOpen (www.springeropen.com) where articles are peer reviewed and of the same production quality as their print-based, subscription-only journals. While there is a charge for publishing in these journals, the charges are sometimes lowered in certain cases. The charges may also be waived for authors from countries with lower incomes and, for some of their journals, postgraduate students who are submitting work to the journal (see http://languagetestingasia.springeropen.com/submission-guidelines/fees-and-funding for more on this). It is, then, most certainly worth considering open access journals if the aim and focus of the journal has a good fit with your paper.

The Role of Social Media in Academic Journal Publishing

Publishers are increasingly using social media to increase both the visibility and connectivity of their journals. Elsevier, Springer, Taylor & Francis, and Wiley-Blackwell, for example, all have Twitter accounts that they regularly use to let people know about their latest issues. They also use Facebook for a similar purpose. Some authors also use Facebook to let people know about their publications. Sites such as ResearchGate (www.researchgate.net), Academia.edu (www.academia.edu), and Figshare (figshare.com) are especially dedicated to this purpose, allowing authors to list their published work and, if the publisher of the work allows, place copies of their articles on the site. ResearchGate also has a feature through which people can ask an author for a copy of his or her article, often described as an e-print, which can be sent to them directly without having to place the article formally on the website. ResearchGate also allows researchers to post questions they would like answers to.

Google Scholar (scholar.google.com) can be used to search for a particular author's work as well as to set up an alert to let you know when your work has been cited. Google Scholar also has a feature through which you can see how often your work has been cited. Sage has developed a site titled Methodspace (www.methodspace.com/) where you can ask questions about research methods, discuss your research with other researchers, and blog about your research.

These are just some of the ways that publishers and authors are using social media within the context of academic publishing. Other ways will no doubt emerge as the affordances of social media evolve.

Judith Bell and Stephen Waters (2014, p. 153), authors of *Doing Your Research Project: A Guide for First Time Researchers*, give this advice on using social media: "Although the potential of social media is unarguable, as with all your research activities you need to manage your time effectively—social media activity can be addictive and hours can slip by unnoticed." This is advice we would very much agree with.

Targeting Academic Journals

Targeting particular journals for submission options involves a number of possible strategies. One thing to do is determine the journals that the more well-regarded authors in your field are publishing in. Do this by looking at the work you have cited by these authors in your own writing or in an article you are currently reading. Look also at state-of-the-art chapters or review articles on your topic in handbooks and encyclopedias to see which journals most frequently appear. Additionally, search your topic on Google Scholar and look at the reference lists of highly cited articles on your topic. The key authors in your field may, of course, publish across a range of journals, but this search can give you a good starting point for finding journals that might publish your article.

It is important to read a range of journals to get an idea of the articles each publishes and whether the article you are writing will fit with the kinds of papers that appear in the journal. There has to be a match between the orientation of the project you are reporting on (such as quantitative, qualitative, mixed methods) and the kinds of articles the journal typically publishes—that is, whether your paper uses numeric data and statistics (a typical feature of quantitative studies), whether it uses data such as interviews and observations (methods that are often used in qualitative studies), or whether it combines both quantitative and qualitative data (a key feature of mixed methods studies). Your article also needs to be on a topic that the journal typically publishes.

Look carefully at the information for authors on the journals' websites; these are usually very clear about what kinds of articles each journal publishes. Review this information and highlight everything related to your article. If there are no connections between the information and the focus of your article, look further into the journal to see if the journal has published anything on your topic written from the perspective with which you are working.

Another strategy to employ when targeting journals is to read the editorials because these often give clues as to what the journal is looking for, what the hot topics are, and what kinds of articles the journal generally considers.

Brian was inspired by a comment in an editorial in the journal in which his 1992 article appeared that said that some of the most interesting work was happening in what some people, at the time, might have considered somewhat peripheral locations. He was working in a very new institution in a small town in New Zealand then. The institution was extremely well funded, and faculty members were given complete freedom to develop programs as they wished. Motivated by the editor's comment, he wrote an article about the test for placing new students that he had developed for this institution. He thought it may have been of interest to the wide readership of the journal. As it turned out, it was, and it was published.

You should also look at the editorial boards for journals to see whether the people on the board have published on your topic or you have cited them in your paper. If they are all (or mostly) people whose work you are familiar with, this is an indication that you may be looking in the right place. If you do not know the work of any of the people on the board, this perhaps suggests that while the title of the journal might seem like a good place for you to send your article, the journal's take on the topic might be quite different from yours and not be a suitable place to send your article.

Evaluating Potential Journals

A number of factors will help you evaluate potential journals and guide your decision as to where you submit your article. First, audience is key. Who do you want to read your work? Is it other researchers, practitioners, or the general public? Next is the quality and focus of articles in the journal and how this compares with your assessment of the quality and focus of your article. Third is how the journal is perceived in your field in terms of its quality and ranking.

Some years ago, Brian moved to an academic position in a city he had not lived in before. He had published well in international journals but wanted to get known by the local language teaching community as that was his area of specialization. To do this, he submitted an article to a local teachers' publication about practical aspects of his research, even though he knew it would not count in his institution as his other publications would. The article was only based on a small number of data extracts so would not have been considered for a high-ranking academic journal. As a result of publishing in the teachers' journal, however, he was subsequently invited to speak to teacher groups and at a local language teachers' conference, which is exactly what he was hoping would happen.

Is the Journal Peer Reviewed?

A key issue is whether the journal is peer reviewed. This, however, can sometimes be harder to determine than it might seem. There may or may not be a statement to this effect on the journal's website.

If the journal has an editorial board or an annual list of reviewers that are thanked/acknowledged, however, you can then assume that it is peer reviewed.

What Is the Standing of the Publisher?

The standing of the publisher is a further consideration—that is, whether it is published by a well-established publishing house, a university press, or a society or association that has a strong reputation in the field. Large publishing houses such as Elsevier, Springer, Taylor & Francis, Wiley-Blackwell, and Sage publish many academic journals. Elsevier, for example, publishes 2,500 journals (Elsevier, 2015a), Springer 2,200 journals (Springer, n.d.), Taylor & Francis 1,600 journals (Taylor & Francis, 2015), Wiley-Blackwell 1,500 journals (Wiley, 2015), and Sage 750 journals (Sage, 2015). Elsevier, Springer, Taylor & Francis, Wiley-Blackwell, and Sage also publish journals in association with international scholarly and professional associations. Oxford University Press publishes more than 360 journals (Oxford University Press, 2015), Cambridge University Press more than 300 journals (Cambridge University Press, 2015), the University of Chicago Press 60 journals (University of Chicago Press, n.d.), and the University of California Press 55 journals (University of California Press, 2015). Associations such as the American Psychological Association and IEEE (the Institute of Electrical and Electronics Engineers) also publish many well regarded articles in their fields of research and are equally high regarded. Each of these publishers has a well-established publishing reputation and peer review process. As a result, the journals they publish are usually positively regarded by academic institutions, although matters such as impact factors, acceptance rates, the reputation of the editor(s) and authors who publish in the journal, and the quality of the content of the journal also influence how they are viewed (Wellington & Torgerson, 2005). And, of course, all of this is dominated by English language publications that, unfortunately, are often given higher status than journals published in other languages (see Lillis & Curry, 2010, for a discussion of this).

How Long Has the Journal Been Published and What Is Its Quality of Production?

It is also important to establish how long the journal has been published because this is an indication that it has established a place in the field. You can determine this by looking at the number of volumes that have been produced. You also want to see if the journal is carefully produced. With the increase in new online journals, quality is becoming an issue since it is relatively easy to put material online, and not all of the journals are as carefully produced as they should be. You can determine how current the journal is from its website. If the most recent issue is a few years old, this suggests the journal may not publish regularly. When an issue is published, the articles will already be dated, and it will take time for people to see your article.

Who Publishes in the Journal?

You should also look at who publishes in the journal, especially whether people with standing in the field are represented. Another point to look out for is whether only members of the journal's editorial board are published in the journal. If they are, this suggests the journal may not be a good place for you to send your article.

What Is the Visibility and Accessibility of the Journal?

You also want to get a sense of the visibility and accessibility of the journal. For example, is the journal available online or through a library, or does it require you to have membership of a particular association in order to access it? If the journal is difficult for you to access, it will be just as hard for other people to access, meaning that it might be difficult for everyone you want to see your work to find it.

Does the Journal Have Themed or Special Issues?

One other possibility is to find out if the journal you are interested in has an upcoming theme or special issue on your topic. Be cautious, however, as from our experience, special issues can be less predictable than you might imagine. The articles in a special issue typically go through the same peer review process as other submissions to the journal; if too few articles pass the submission process, there may be no special issue! On the other hand, if the articles that have been submitted for a special issue require more work than regular articles submitted to the journal, the editor(s) of the special issue may be happy to work with you, more than would normally be the case, to get your article to the required standard. We have seen both these situations in our journal editing experience.

What Is the Word or Page Limit for Articles?

A further issue to be aware of is the word or page limit for submissions to the journal and whether that fits with your article. Some journals, such as *Nature*, may have an upper word limit of 3,000 words, whereas in other journals articles may be up to 7,500 words (for example, the *Journal of Philosophy*). Some journals such as *Cognition* may have no word limit at all.

Deciding Which Journal Fits Your Article

Figure 2.1 is a worksheet we ask students to complete to help them make a decision about the journals that would be most suited for their article and to what extent their article might fit with these journals. It also helps them clarify matters such as the style guide for the journal and how the article should be submitted.

=== **Figure 2.1** ===

Worksheet for Evaluating Academic Journals

	Journal 1	Journal 2	Journal 3
Name of the journal			
Is the journal peer reviewed?			
Who is the publisher of the journal?			
Who is the audience for the journal?			
What type of journal is it (disciplinary, field-based, regional, etc.)?			
Do key people in your field publish in the journal?			
How long has the journal been published?			
How accessible is the journal?			
What is the journal's quality of production?			
How should articles be submitted?			
What is the word or page limit for submissions to the journal?			

Internationalizing a Research Article

A key issue a new writer needs to consider is the relevance of his or her research to the international readership of the journal to which he or she wishes to submit the article. This is crucial for you to address when submitting an article to a peer-reviewed journal. Many writers, not just those that are new to academic publishing, find it difficult to frame their research so that it will be of interest to a wider, more international readership of a journal. It is essential, however, that they do this. Here's an example to illustrate the point.

Imagine you have written a research article on ways to stop diseases among fish on the fish farms in your country. In order to make the research acceptable to an international audience, you are considering these options:

1. You internationalize the literature review by referring to research carried out in other parts of the world on your topic in the Literature Review and by discussing your work in relation to this research in the Discussion section of your article.

2. You focus on the one fish species (such as tilapia) that is widely grown in fish farms across the world.

3. You contact an author in another part of the world working on the same problem and suggest combining data and co-authoring the article.

4. You explain more clearly why fish farming is so important for your country's economy.

Each of these proposed solutions has pros and cons. Some of these should be addressed regardless of the final audience for the article. For example, the literature review (Point 1) should be internationalized regardless of which journal the article will be sent to. Point 2, focusing on the one fish species that is widely grown in fish farms across the world, is probably a stronger option than Point 3, because this option could lead to two very local discussions that are still not especially internationalized. Point 4, like Point 1, is something that should be done no matter who the audience for the journal is since it is a key point to justify the research.

Keys to Publishing Success

In order to succeed in getting published, it is important to understand the aims, orientation, and expectations of the journal you wish to publish in and be certain that the work you are submitting fits it. Your article also needs to conform to the specifications given in the journal's Notes for Authors. This is something many writers do not do. Indeed, some editors will not consider an article if the author has not followed the journal's guidelines (see Chapter 3 for further discussion of this). It is also important that you follow how the journal wants the article to be presented. For example, does it require a particular font and format? How are figures and tables to be submitted? Often journals require these to be submitted as separate files with "Place Figure 1 here" in the text.

Finally, don't expect the journal to be an editing service or that the editor will correct mistakes in language use or find missing references. It is your responsibility to make sure the text is in good clear English and that all the necessary references are listed and that they

We often, prior to final acceptance, have to do a lot of copyediting of articles to get them ready to send to the publisher. With the journal Sue edited, she received page proofs of articles to double check before they were published. Brian's journal does not send him page proofs. Proofs only go to the author and to the publisher's copyeditor. This means that any final editing by the editor has to be done before the article is formally accepted for publication. This may mean communicating with an author to check on some details or it may be things the editor can deal with himself. These two situations illustrate that you cannot always assume that an editor will have seen the final page proofs of your article, so it is really important you check the page proofs if they are sent to you. And you should be sure to respond to requests for changes to the proofs as quickly as you can so that your article is not held up at this stage of the process. And, of course, you don't want your article appearing with mistakes in it.

are correct. An untidy article will not help your chances of getting published.

It is a good idea for writers who are new to this kind of publishing to ask someone to read the article to check for language problems. If you are a non-native speaker of English, this is especially important. While many published authors of journal articles (and editors of academic journals) are non-native speakers, it is equally important that you do not let language issues affect what you want to say or give an editor who is overwhelmed with submissions an excuse to reject your manuscript (see Chapter 5 for more on this topic).

Don't Be Discouraged

A final, important point to make is to not be discouraged by what seems to be the very high standing of a journal. While he was still working on his PhD, Brian read the following comment by Ros Mitchell who was, at the time, one of editors of a highly ranked journal in his field. She said, "It is important to bear in mind that a rejection from one journal doesn't mean your paper is unpublishable. . . . Rejection is common, it is normal, it is frequent, and [it] by no means means that the paper won't find a home somewhere else" (BAAL, 1993, p. 10–11). This comment encouraged Brian to submit an article to the journal that Mitchell was editing that drew on his dissertation-in-process, knowing that if it didn't succeed there he could always send it to the next journal on his list. As it was, the article was accepted and published in Mitchell's journal. He also later learned that one of his reviewers had been the current editor of a journal in the more specific part of the field in which he was researching. As years went by, he met this reviewer at a conference who then began to invite him to review for his journal. At a later stage, he invited Brian to be a member of the editorial board for the journal. Some years after that, Brian was invited to be editor of the journal itself. None of this would have happened to Brian had he not taken Mitchell's words to heart.

Chapter 3

Connecting Your Article to Readers

In this chapter, we discuss some of the common problems that authors have making their article as reader friendly as possible. Some solutions are presented as well.

Think about your potential readers: they are, first, the editor, then the reviewers, and then others in your field. Academics are busier and busier and have less time for reading, and there are also more and more journals competing for readers' time. Online publication has facilitated the diffusion of academic publications but contributed to the proliferation of easily accessible articles. Communicating clearly about your research and presenting it in formats that meet a reader's expectations is vital.

Journal publishers have invested in researching how readers interact with journals and articles online. Today, most journals publish very few hard copies. This is because journal publishers know that the norm is for readers to search online and that few readers read an issue of a journal through from beginning to end. Based on information provided by journal publishers over several years, we know that most readers tend to search online using keywords or click through from another article or a Contents Alert email. Obviously, the more you can do as a writer to help readers locate your article online, the more readers will read your article.

We recently were excited to have an article accepted in a journal published by a well-known publisher. We received a message from the publisher encouraging us to make use of a new online feature to make sure our article "gets the attention it deserves." The new feature allows authors to put together a PowerPoint presentation, with audio, about their research that is uploaded next to the published article. We know about other journals that invite authors to create a small video presentation on their research that can be uploaded to the publisher's website. In today's crowded research jungle, there are greater expectations of authors in terms of promoting their research and more opportunities for them to do this.

Choosing Keywords

Choosing keywords is important in several ways. Keywords are used to help the editor(s) find potential reviewers. Most journals have online databases of reviewers, and the reviewers identify the areas they are able to review in. When authors upload their articles, they identify which of those areas their work falls within and assignments are made. Authors are also typically asked to identify four or five keywords, which do not have to be single words—they can be short phrases. If the editor decides to send an article out for review, the keywords and the areas selected are used by the editor to identify reviewers. Therefore, the more your keywords match with key terms used in your field, the greater the likelihood that the reviewer will understand your work.

The Importance of a Good Title

Take time to think carefully about your title because it is the first thing that will attract readers. Once you've selected the journal you plan to submit to, look through the most recent issues of the journal and quickly analyze the article titles. Since the articles were published, these titles obviously were successful. As you read through the titles, ask yourself these questions:

- ❑ From a title alone, do you get a clear sense of what the article is about?
- ❑ Does the title make you want to read the article?
- ❑ Does the title make the aims of the article clear?
- ❑ Does the title give a clue about the approach used in the research?
- ❑ Does the title communicate what the original contribution of the article may be?
- ❑ How long are the titles? Work out the average word length. Some journals may provide guidelines. Be sure you check.
- ❑ Do the titles have two parts—that is, before and after a colon? What is the general tendency in the journal?
- ❑ Do the titles contain quotes from the data? If so, how common is this?
- ❑ Do the titles pose a question?

First impressions do count. Sometimes we can see from its title that the article is not going to be a good fit for the journal we are editing. For example, as editor of *English for Specific Purposes*, Sue might see the word *English* in a title but think that none of the other words in the title relate to any of the journal's concerns. Often these article are about English literature, which is not an area of interest for her journal. From her experience, she knows that these types of articles are likely to become "desk rejects." (See page 72 for further discussion of desk rejections.)

As a general rule, a shorter title is probably better than a longer title, but be guided by the prevailing style of the journal and what you notice. Bear in mind too that most articles are found these days by keyword searching, so having at least some of your keywords in your title can help readers find your work. It might also be a good idea to put your proposed title into Google just to see if it closely matches any other titles. You can always change yours slightly to differentiate it.

Above all, don't waste your title. It is a valuable resource for communicating what the key focus of your article is, initially to the editor, then to reviewers, and then to your readers.

When Brian first started publishing, he was keen to establish a reputation as someone with expertise in the area of genre studies. As a result, many of his early articles had the word *genre* in the title. On one occasion, however, he used the word *genre* in the title of an article when it was not really about genre, but about discourse interpretation. Not surprisingly, the article was sent to reviewers in the area of genre analysis, one of whom said "This article is not about genre!" and recommended rejection of the article (which the editor agreed with). The reviewer was, of course, right. Brian revised the article, removing the focus on genre, and sent it to another journal where, after revisions, it was published.

Writing a Successful Abstract

Once you've completed your analysis of journal article titles, look at the abstracts of the articles whose titles made you want to read them. The purpose of the abstract is to enable readers to quickly decide whether they want to read the whole article. Once you have submitted your article to your chosen journal, the first readers of your abstract will be the editors, and if they decide to send it out for review, the next readers will be the two or three reviewers who will decide, on the basis of your abstract and the title, whether to accept or decline the invitation to review your article.

Most journals make abstracts freely available online, so scholars searching online are likely to read your abstract before deciding whether to download the article. Also, electronic Content Alerts that you can sign up for with the journals you commonly read will enable you to click through to the abstract and view it without charge. You can understand, therefore, why the abstract is an important component of the article. The abstract needs to provide a clear and concise overview of your article. It should indicate the aims of the research, situate it within the context of previous research, indicate the approach you took to carry out the study, and note what your key findings were. Importantly—and something we find is often missing—your abstract should indicate how your study contributes to the area you are studying. Be sure to include some of your keywords in your abstract to help readers searching in your topic area. The journal you are targeting should provide information on its website about how long the abstract should be. Please stick to the required word length. If no word length is given, then we advise you to keep the abstract between 250–300 words.

Many writers have been told to write the abstract once the article is completed. However, based on our experience, we recommend drafting the abstract early in the process to provide you with a road map of the structure of your article. The abstract may change over time as your thinking evolves, but it should still provide a basic framework.

As editors, we have quite often found that the abstract is clear and well-argued but that the article itself doesn't follow the logic of the abstract. It's easy to lose your way in an 8,000-word article, so use your abstract as a way of checking what will be included in the article.

In our writing-for-publication workshops, we often ask participants to use Brown's 8 Questions when drafting an abstract (see Brown, 1994). The recommended time for this exercise is 30 minutes. We ask participants to notice that two of the questions explicitly ask them to think about the readers of the article and what the benefit for readers will be. We recommend taking the time to seriously think about the questions, adhere to the word limits, and draft responses in full sentences. Brown's 8 Questions are listed:

1. Who are the intended readers? List 3–5 by name.

2. What did you do? (50 words)

3. Why did you do it? (50 words)

4. What happened (when you did that)? (50 words)

5. What do the results mean in theory? (50 words)

6. What do the results mean in practice? (50 words)

7. What is the key benefit for readers? (25 words)

8. What remains unresolved? (no word limit)

Abstracts and the Writing of Abstracts by John Swales and Christine Feak (2009) is a very helpful book on writing the different kinds of abstracts that scholars need to write, including journal article abstracts. However, their book does not include some of the newer types of abstracts that are emerging in the online journal world such as graphical abstracts, video abstracts, and research highlights. Many journal publishers now encourage authors, depending on their field, to upload a graphical representation of the abstract or a list of the article's main points in dot points (research highlights). As we mentioned earlier, journals may also provide an opportunity to upload a video abstract. *Cell Press,* publisher of a number of biological journals, provides examples of video abstracts online (www.cell.com/video-abstract-guidelines).

Variation in the Structure of Journal Articles

As editors, one of the most important bits of advice we can give to authors is to read the journal's guidelines to authors and to do as they say! Although journal articles all have the same components, across journals there are many variations; article length, formatting, and reference style can all vary considerably, journal to journal. While not adhering to the journal's guidelines may not lead to your article's rejection, it could result in it being sent back to you and putting you at the end of the publishing queue (see Chapter 4).

When we think of the typical structure of a journal article, and what most readers will expect, we tend to immediately think of the standard Introduction–Methods–Results–Discussion (IMRD) structure. While this is a common pattern of organization in many fields, recent research has identified variations on this pattern. A study (Lin & Evans, 2012) of the organizational patterns of 433 empirical research articles across 39 disciplines from high-impact English language journals found that the IMRD pattern, while still a major organizational pattern, was not the default option for most articles. The

The website for Sue's journal clearly stated that articles should be between 6,000 and 8,000 words. Many authors did not consult the guidelines or chose to ignore them. Authors who sent in articles of 3,000 and 4,000 words were, nearly without exception, going to be immediately rejected because with so few words, the article likely did not contain sufficient evidence of original research. If an article was between 10,000 and 12,000 words, or even longer, but the topic was within the journal's scope, Sue would write to the authors to request that they shorten it to meet the journal's word limit. A word limit of 8,000 words is reasonable. Authors should be able to communicate research findings within that limit. Also, as we say elsewhere in this book, reviewers are very busy people, and reviewing an article takes time, so editors try to not overburden them. So particularly when writing from a dissertation or thesis where you may have lengthy chapters, find out what the journal's maximum word length is and stick to that.

more typical pattern was actually Introduction–Literature Review–Methods–Results and Discussion–Conclusion (ILM[RD]C) (the square brackets indicate that the Results and Discussion section are merged). They also found that just over 50 percent of the articles had a distinct Literature Review section between the Introduction and the Methods section and that another fairly common pattern was Introduction–Methods–Results and Discussion–Conclusion (IM[RD]C). In terms of Results and Discussion sections, Lin and Evans (2012) found that these sections were merged in 39.3 percent of the articles examined, while 49.2 percent had a separate Results section and 51.5 percent had a separate Discussion section.

As Lin and Evans (2012) point out in reference to their study, the advice in many style guides and writing manuals may not provide new scholars with sufficient information about the options available to them when organizing a journal article. The most important factor is disciplinary variation. What is crucial for new scholars, then, is to look carefully at the format of the articles in the journal they have chosen and to be aware that there is more than one way to structure a research article. The structure or organization of journal articles is not cast in stone. As this new research reveals, over time, the typical structural patterns of research articles do evolve.

The most influential factor in how journal articles in your field are structured will be how they have traditionally been structured. Reviewers and editors will have an expectation of how research findings are to be presented, and if your presentation differs significantly from what they are expecting, they will notice and will examine your work more carefully. This does not mean you have to slavishly adhere to typical formats. However, being aware that there are typical patterns may facilitate the progress of your article. The journal's website may provide explicit guidelines regarding section headings and formatting. Consult the guidelines and follow them. The journal editors will appreciate this, and you will be considered a responsible writer!

If there are no explicit guidelines for the journal, look at articles in the three most recent issues of the journal and answer these questions:

❑ What are the main headings of the articles?

❑ How standard is the usage of these headings?

❑ How long are the different sections under each heading?

❑ Are the headings more generic (e.g., Literature Review, Methods, Results, Discussion, etc.) or more thematic?

Creating a Research Space

Colleagues regularly tell us that writing the Introduction and Discussion sections are the most challenging. This is most likely because it is in these two sections that authors have to situate their own research in relation to the broader field and then create a space for their own research by discussing it in relation to existing research in the field. Whether explicitly titled Introduction or not, all articles will begin with a section that introduces the key aims of the research to the reader, relates the current research to concerns in the field more broadly, and suggests why the research is important in some way. In the words of Feak and Swales (2011, p. xiii), you are "creat[ing] a writing context" for your research.

Feak and Swales (2011) further explain that readers tend not to read articles in a linear fashion, or straight through from introduction to conclusion. As we might expect, busy readers tend to start with the Introduction and then move directly on to the Discussion section as they are keen to discover how the aims set out in your Introduction have been realized. So, it is important to make sure that these two sections clearly link to one another.

Research article Introductions across diverse disciplines have been found to have a typical organizational pattern through which scholars try to communicate that their topic is worthy of study. The busy reader of your article will have certain expectations about the structure of your introduction.

The work of John Swales (1990, 2004) has been very influential in helping us understand the typical organization of introductory sections. Swales called the framework he developed *Creating a Research Space (CaRS)* because he saw this as the key function of the Introduction in a journal article. He examined a large number of journal article Introductions and found a typical pattern in which authors justify the need for their study through what he called *moves*. A *move* refers to a unit of text that functions to communicate the writer's meaning to a reader. He identified three moves in empirically oriented journal article introductions (see Table 3.1). Knowledge about these moves can help authors of research articles better structure their introductions to meet reader expectations.

Notice that Move 1b, introducing and reviewing items of previous research, is obligatory in research papers. Your readers will expect your article to contain a comprehensive review of relevant literature on your topic. If you do not do this, you may get a desk rejection from the editor with a message such as this:

> I am afraid your article is not sufficiently located within current scholarship for a research article in our journal. Readers (and reviewers) would expect the literature on which research articles are based to be as up-to-date and state-of-the-art as possible, which, I am afraid, is not the case with your submission.

=== **Table 3.1** ===

3 Moves in Empirical Research Article Introductions

1. Establishing a research territory
   a. showing that the general research area is important, central, interesting, problematic, or relevant in some way (optional)
   b. introducing and reviewing items of previous research in the area (obligatory)

2. Establishing a niche (citations to previous literature possible)
   a. indicating a gap in the previous research
   b. extending previous knowledge in some way

3. Presenting the present work (citations to previous literature possible)
   a. outlining its purposes or stating the nature of the present research (obligatory)
   b. listing the research questions or hypotheses (probable in some fields but rare in others)
   c. announcing the principal findings (probable in some fields but rare in others)
   d. stating the value of the present research (probable in some fields but rare in others)
   e. indicating the structure of the article (probable in some fields but rare in others)

Source: Feak, C. B., & J. M. Swales, *Creating Contexts: Writing Introductions across Genres.* University of Michigan Press, 2011, p. 55. Used with permission.

Move 2 is obviously important because it is where you signal the gap in the previous research referred to in Move 1. While not all research reports will necessarily indicate that something is missing, you need to indicate that your research is building on previous research.

Move 3 is important because it is where you explain how your study makes a contribution to the field, particularly in Move 3d—stating the value of the present research—although, as Table 3.1 shows, this move is not present in all fields. Research into the structure of journal article Introductions does suggest that "promotional elements" are becoming more common (Martín & León Pérez, 2014, p. 1). According to Martín and León Pérez, Moves 3c and 3d are used by writers in a number of fields "explicitly highlighting the novel contribution that their work makes to the discipline" (p. 2).

They do point out, however, that both the language background of the authors and disciplinary preferences may play a role in writers' decisions as whether to use these two Moves. Martín and León Pérez (2014) found that the articles they examined from Spanish language journals tended to have fewer instances of promotional language than did their English language counterparts in similar subfields. This difference may be attributable to there being less competition to get published in the Spanish-speaking world than in the English language publishing world.

Writers who have previously published solely in a language other than English should therefore carefully examine the Introductions of English language articles in their fields to see to what extent promotional strategies are in place. Deciding how much to "promote" one's work can be difficult to figure out. Our best advice is to examine the writing of other scholars in the journal that you would like to publish in.

Similarly, other research has examined the prevalence of Move 2 in which a research gap is identified in articles written in languages other than English. Hirano (2009) compared articles written in English and in Brazilian Portuguese within the same disciplinary area. She found that 70 percent of the articles in Brazilian Portuguese did not contain a Move 2 and, therefore, did not establish a research niche. In fact three of the articles only contained a single Move—either Move 1 or Move 3. All but one of the English language articles on the other hand, regardless of the country of origin of the author, contained a Move 2 and more than one move. Studies carried out on articles written in Thai and Malay also reported that a proportion of the articles did not have a Move 2 (Jogthong, 2001; Ahmad 1997). Hirano believes that the absence of Move 2 in the articles she examined is due to a desire not to be seen to be "finding fault with the Brazilian research" (p. 246) community. As this community would be smaller than an international one, this seems to be a plausible explanation. The lack of a Move 2 may also be due to the difficulties that researchers in developing countries experience when trying to access research published elsewhere.

Whatever the reason for an absence of a clear "research niche," it seems that reviewers and readers of English language journals have an expectation that Introductions will create a research space using a

Move 2. The absence of this move may lead to writers from language backgrounds other than English struggling to have their research favorably reviewed. Writers who have published in their first language and are not accustomed to the CaRS framework may wish to consider adopting it as it seems to depict a frequently used way of communicating in scholarly English.

While the examples provided of the potential difference between English and other languages in terms of variances in the CaRS framework may not, strictly speaking, be language related, they do suggest that language can be playing a role in writing for publication for non–English speaking authors.

When we teach writing-for-publication courses, we use the CaRS model. We ask students to read through the introduction to an article they are working on to see which moves they have included. If there are some they haven't used, then they think about whether it would be useful to add them to their introduction. Try this with an article you are writing. Our students say they have found it very helpful.

The Importance of the Discussion Section

Feak and Swales (2011) point out that many readers of journal articles go straight to the Discussion section and only read other sections if there is sufficient content or information that is new and relevant to their own research. A well-structured Discussion section should therefore be an essential component of your submission. However, many submissions we have received in our time as journal editors omit the Discussion section. New authors, in particular, commonly submit articles that do not include a Discussion section or, if they do, the Discussion section does not do what it is expected to do—that is, does not show how the research article moves the field forward.

In a Discussion section, authors typically refer to many sources as they review the results of their study in relation to previous research. They may also refer to the same piece of research a number of times as they show how their research builds and expands on, or contradicts, earlier research. The Discussion section may also refer to methodological and theoretical sources as it reviews the project that has been reported on. The key function of the Discussion section, therefore, is to clearly indicate to your reader in what ways your study is contributing to the field. You do this by comparing your findings to previous work either to show how previous work supports your findings or how your work distinguishes itself from previous studies. Whereas in the Literature Review, you reviewed previous work in your field in order to establish your research space or gap, in the Discussion section you are now in a position to show how your work contributes to the field.

You show your contribution by making claims about your findings; the data you have collected and analyzed and presented now becomes evidence that supports your claims for the significance of your findings. As in the case of Introduction sections previously discussed, similar research has put forward a typical move organization for Discussion sections (see Table 3.2). The list of typical moves in a Discussion section encapsulates the key functions of the section. While there are several more possible moves in the Discussion section than in the Introduction, they may not necessarily all be present. Note how reference to previous research and explanation become key features of the Discussion (Move 3). We recommend that you use Table 3.2 to analyze the Discussion sections of articles in the journal you have selected for submission of your article. Not all articles will

Table 3.2
The Typical Structure of a Research Article in the Discussion Section

Move 1—Background information (research purposes, theory, methodology)	Optional, but probable in some disciplines
Move 2—Summarising and reporting key results	Obligatory
Move 3—Commenting on the key results (making claims, explaining the results, comparing the new work with the previous studies, offering alterative explanations)	Obligatory
Move 4—Stating the limitations of the study	Optional, but probable in some disciplines
Move 5—Making recommendations for future implementation and/or future research	Optional

Source: Swales, J. M., & C. B. Feak, *Academic Writing for Graduate Students, 3rd ed.* University of Michigan Press, 2012, p. 368. Used with permission.

necessarily have a section clearly headed Discussion, but you should be able to locate that part of the article where the author is discussing the results or findings and comparing them to previous research in the field.

Another key function of the Discussion section is captured by Move 3 in Table 3.2 in which claims are made for the author's research based on the evidence provided by the data. Reviewers tend to look very carefully at the type of claims authors make. They make statements such as *the author should explain why . . . .* and *I think that some of the claims in the article need to be better supported, for example.* So authors need to be fairly cautious when making claims for the significance of their findings and not overstate their claims. This is why it often becomes necessary to *hedge,* or soften, the strength of claims we make as academic authors. We need to ask ourselves questions such as:

❑ Is there enough evidence to support my claim?

❑ Am I overgeneralizing?

Table 3.3 offers some language authors can use to strengthen or weaken the claims in their Discussion sections. There are many other ways authors can use language to do this, and we recommend that new authors study the Discussion sections of journal articles in their fields to better understand how to make claims that reviewers and editors will find credible.

Table 3.3
Language That Makes Claims Weaker or Stronger

Weaker	Making Claims ◄————————►	Stronger
might result in	*may result in*	*will result in*
it is possible that	*it is very likely/probable that*	*it is certain that*
would seem to have	*seem to have*	*have*
may have contributed to	*contributed to*	*caused*
suggests	*indicates*	*shows*

A common question we get asked by our students is whether the Results and Discussion sections need to be separate or if they can be combined. As our reference to Lin and Evans' (2012) study shows, there is no simple yes or no answer to this question. Lin and Evans point out that whatever you do, you need to understand the difference between each of these sections. The Results section, they point out, "focuses on new knowledge and aims to convert findings into textual form" (p. 157) whereas the Discussion section makes connections between the new knowledge and previous research in the field. The Discussion section also "offers possible explanations for the findings and occasionally make claims about the contribution, limitations and future avenues of the research" (p. 157). Whichever way you choose to structure your article, you need to both say what your new knowledge is and connect it to previous research on your topic, regardless of whether you separate or merge the Results and Discussion sections.

When we look at reviewers' feedback on submitted articles, the importance of clearly illustrating how an author's research is adding to the field comes through strongly. Here are some anonymous comments in which the reviewers point to the need for the author to highlight what his or her research is adding to the field:

> I worry that I see little difference between prior literature and your study, especially in terms of the theoretical contribution. How institutional, resource dependence, and resource-based factors directly affect strategic responses has been examined before, demonstrated by the several cited studies in theory section. Thus, one could argue that . . . combining several theories might not be a significant theoretical contribution. That is, the combination does not advance our current understanding much. To further develop your model and offer a greater theoretical contribution, I suggest that you elaborate theory section in greater detail.

> In the reviewer's opinion the article unfortunately does not really add to the existing literature either in theory or in practice.

This is a very well-written piece, with something original and interesting to say. The intent of the article is clear, aspects of it are well expressed and relevant examples are brought to bear on the phenomena being considered. However, I regret having to say that I do not see what is actually being added in terms of an understanding of the area itself, or in providing a really new practice or approach in aid of finding resolutions which were not already known, and that had not already been applied to achieve what would appear to be the same result the authors believe their approach would generate.

The issue of what is new in the field seems to be uppermost in reviewers' minds. We have also seen reviewers raise questions about well-written and well-researched articles because they feel the topic has been overresearched, meaning they believe there is nothing more to say about it, and that they are tired of reading articles on it. So while a topic has to connect to previous research in the field, it should also have something **new** to offer and not simply replicate previous studies. It is also important, as we point out, to tell your reader in what way your research is novel (see Move 3d, Table 3.1).

Do I Need a Separate Conclusion?

As Lin and Evans' (2012) study found, empirical articles with separate Conclusion sections have become reasonably common. Journals tend to have different traditions in this regard, so once again we advise you to examine recent volumes of the journal you are submitting to and identify the dominant organizational pattern. If you decide to have a separate concluding section, then Move 5 (Making recommendations) from Table 3.2 would become part of the Conclusion section. Part of what is generally done in the Conclusion section is to identify new "knowledge deficits" (Giltrow, 2005, p. 259); that is, explicitly identify what is still not known in the field, which could lead to further research either by yourself or someone else. In a concluding section, you would likely also discuss any limitations to your study.

Most important, the concluding section is where you discuss the implications of your research, and these differ depending on the kind of research you have done. For example, your study could have implications for policy, for practice, for theory, or for some other area that is relevant to your field. What is important is that you indicate where the contribution of your study lies. Janet Giltrow (2005, p. 259) sees the conclusion as being the "writer's last chance to make sure that connections between parts of the discussion are secure in readers' minds ... [and] to invoke the complex, high-level abstractions which motivated the discussion, made sense of its specifics, and contributed to the scholarly conversation."

Giltrow (2005, p. 260) also suggests considering the person reading the conclusion. She suggests that he or she is a *"different reader* [italics in original] from the one who read your introduction." By the end of the article (if it was read in a linear manner), your reader "has encountered detailed analysis and illustration, the claims and supporting evidence." The reader needs to be reminded of "key abstractions and important findings" that confirm your claims to significance. Of course, in reality, the reader is the same person as the one who began reading your article. What Giltrow wants you to think about is how, in the light of what they now know, readers may be reading and understanding your conclusion.

The conclusions you make in your article need to be related to the questions posed in the Introduction and to the discussion of the findings/interpretations used to answer these questions. Whereas the questions are the main focus of the Introduction, the answers are the main focus of the conclusion. Readers don't expect to find new information in the Conclusion section. When an article did that, here is what one reviewer stated: "A whole lot of new material is introduced into the conclusion—a lot of this would be more useful in the body of the article to build on the findings as they are presented."

The Importance of Current References

One of the first things editors and reviewers look at is the reference list that accompanies the article. When Brian gets a new submission, he immediately looks at the reference list to see how up to date the sources are. If there are no references to articles published in the last five years, he then looks to see how current the research is that is referred to in the article. Showing that you are in touch with current conversations in the field is important. This is especially important if you are publishing from your PhD that was completed some time ago. Also, make sure to discuss new research in your article. It is not just a matter of adding more recent references. You need to show that you know what current research has to say about your topic.

Having a reference list in the correct format—whether APA, MLA, Harvard, Vancouver, or Chicago—can help ensure the smooth passage of your article through the review process. Editors get irritated when authors have not bothered to follow the appropriate format and guidelines listed on the website, especially when there is now software to do it for you!

Reading as a Writer

Throughout this chapter, we have emphasized how important it is for you to be a responsible writer. One of the most useful tips we can give you is to read like a writer. Mostly we read journal articles for their content. Every now and then, however, it is a good idea to read as a writer as we have suggested throughout this chapter: Read to see how the author of the article you are reading has put the article together. What organizational patterns has the author used, what language resources are drawn on, how has the author pointed out the significance of the study, and has the author hedged (or not) in the claims made?

Chapter 4

Understanding the Peer Review Process

The process of peer review is fundamental to ensuring the quality of published research. The International Committee of Medical Journal Editors (2009) describes peer review as "the critical assessment of manuscripts submitted to journals by experts who are not part of the editorial staff." The reviewers are, as the name suggests, your peers—that is, people working and researching in your area of research. They may be members of the journal's editorial board, or they may be people who are not on the board but who have standing in the field and whose work is well regarded on your particular topic. They may also be graduate students who are doing research in the same area as yours, especially if the person the editor approaches is busy and passes the review on to one of his or her students.

As well as an editor (or editors), journals also have editorial boards who review for the journal and give advice on editorial matters. For some journals, the membership of the editorial board changes on an annual basis with some people rotating off and others coming on. This is the case with the journal that Brian currently edits. In other cases, such as the journal that Sue edited, people stayed on the board much longer. Very often, however, the reviewers will be a mix of editorial board members and other people with expertise on the particular topic.

In order to decide who to ask to review an article, editors consider who is on the board that has expertise on the particular topic. They also look at the research the author has cited to see who has done the most current work on the topic and often approach those individuals to review the article. Editors also look at the journal's database of reviewer expertise, which is a summary of the areas of expertise that have been nominated by previous authors of articles in the journal when they have sent submissions in to the journal. They also consider the keywords the author has chosen for the article to find a match between reviewers and the article. And, of course, editors draw on their own knowledge of who is working in the particular area and who may be interested in reading a submission. Through all this, editors try to find a match, not just between the topic and the reviewer's expertise, but also between the paradigm or approach that the author has used so there is no clash of expectations between what the author has done and what the reviewer expects.

It is through this process of peer review, then, that the quality of the work submitted is vetted (appraised by an expert) and that ultimately determines whether it will or will not be published in the journal. Some people see journal editors as gatekeepers. However, this is only partially true. Reviewers can play as much a part in this as the editor—and sometimes more—especially if the article written is not in the editor's specific area of expertise. In this case, the editor is very much reliant on the views of the reviewers, and it will be their view, rather than that of the editor, that will prevail. This is a situation we have found ourselves in on quite a number of occasions. For example, we may have received an article that, on the surface, looks like a sound piece of research and is on a topic that we like to see covered in the journal. The reviewers, however, may see flaws in the article that we did not and recommend we reject the article. In the end, though, this is what the peer review process is about: getting the views of experts on your topic (who very often are not the editor) and their judgment as to whether your article is a good piece of research within the paradigm or framework with which you are working, and whether it moves the field forward in terms of what we know about the particular topic.

In our experience, articles are always improved once they have been reviewed and the reviewers' comments have been responded to in the revised submission. We say this in relation to the articles we have handled as editors and the articles we have submitted to journals. The role of feedback, thus, is crucial to the production and publication of high-quality articles.

The aim of peer review, then, is to publish the highest quality work as well as to filter out work that has not been well conceived, well designed, or carried out well. Peer review aims to ensure the quality of the research design or methodology of the study and that the work is reported on and interpreted correctly, in relation to other published research on the topic—that it offers something new. Reviewers are typically asked to consider each article in relation to the readership of that journal and to give advice on changes and improvements that should be made to the article so that it is of a standard that is acceptable for publication in the journal. The peer review process, thus, both assesses your work and its quality and provides a mechanism by which you can receive expert feedback on your work and then improve it (see page 76 for typical questions reviewers are asked to consider when assessing submissions).

More specifically, however, the aim of peer review is to ensure that your work is original, valid, and significant (American Psychological Association, 2010). Peer review provides journals with the basis for claims that the work that they publish is of a high standard and is based on good research. Peer review is also an important criterion for the journal to be included in ranking lists such as the *Thomson Reuters Web of Knowledge* (wokinfo.com/about/) database (formerly the ISI—Institute for Scientific Information—index) and its citation reports. Publishing in peer-reviewed journals, thus, is important for both your academic reputation and your career.

The entire system of academic publishing depends on the reciprocal goodwill of scholars who freely give their time and expertise, without remuneration, to review the work of their peers (McPeek et al., 2009). This means that scholars agree to review the work of other scholars with the expectation that these scholars will, in turn, review their work and that of others. Thus, if you have submitted an article to a journal for review, the editor will expect that, at a later date, he or she can ask you to review for the journal. When asked to do this, so long as the article is in your area of expertise, you should agree to do the review.

We are somewhat unimpressed when we invite reviewers whose work we have just published to evaluate a submission and they say no, that they are too busy. If you expect people to read and give you feedback on your work, you also have to be prepared to read and review theirs. We should also add that when we think of people to add to our editorial boards, the first people we think of are those people who have reviewed for us, always agreed when we have asked them, and have sent in thoughtful and fair reviews on time. Doing reviews is a good way to get known by journal editors, which can have benefits for you, beyond just reading the most recent research on your topic. Being a member of a journal's editorial board is good for your career as it is an indication of your standing in the field. Doing reviews of other people's work also has value for your own writing because you can see how other authors have chosen to deal with issues that you have had to deal with in your writing.

Double Blind vs. Single Blind Reviews

Reviewers for academic journals almost always remain anonymous to you, the author. This is called *blind review.* In many cases, the reviewers will not know who you are either. This is called *double blind review.* Even so, reviewers may be able to guess who you are, perhaps because of the topic on which you are writing or the location in which you carried out your research.

Sometimes, however, your name remains on the article that is forwarded to the reviewers. In this case the reviewer knows who you are, but you don't know who the reviewer is. This is called *single blind review.*

Some journals, such has the *British Medical Journal,* use *open peer review.* You will know who your reviewers are, and they will know who you are. Other journals, such as *Nature,* have considered the use of open peer review, but for various reasons have decided not to implement it. One reason given is that it was not popular with the authors or the scientists who were invited to comment on it (*Nature,* 2006).

You should blind your submission if this is a requirement for the particular journal. This will be clearly stated in the journal's guidelines for authors. Blinding an article means that you should take steps to mask your identity in the article so that reviewers will not know who you are. Many authors do not do this. Journal editors will send a submission back to an author if the article has not been blinded.

To blind your article, go through the article and the reference list and change all references to your own work to "Author, 2015" (etc.) with no other details such as the title of the article or chapter, and the name of the journal or book. Then move these references from their current alphabetical place in the reference list, and place them at the top of the reference list as "Author, 2015" (for example) so that your identity cannot be guessed by the placement of the blinded reference in the bibliography. When you do this, you also need to remove the title of the article and journal (or book or book chapter) because you also can be identified from these pieces of information. You should also remove any biographical information and acknowledgments in your text since they can identify you as well. These, and the references to your own work, can be inserted at a later stage if your article is accepted for publication.

Each type of peer review mentioned has advantages and disadvantages. The Elsevier (2015b) website www.elsevier.com/reviewers/what-is-peer-review provides an overview, presented in Table 4.1.

The Role of Editors in the Peer Review Process

Journal editors are typically academics who have high standing in their particular field of research expertise. Some large journals, such as *Nature*, may have full-time salaried editors, but most editors do their journal work at the same time as their other academic work and are not paid for what they do. Or, if they are paid, it may be in the form of a small annual honorarium that they use to attend a conference where an editorial board meeting will be held or to pay for an assistant who can help with some of their editorial work.

Table 4.1

Advantages and Disadvantages of Different Types of Peer Review

Type of Peer Review	Advantages	Disadvantages
Double blind review	Author anonymity prevents reviewer bias based on, for example, an author's country of origin or previous controversial work. Articles written by prestigious or renowned authors are considered on the basis of the content of their articles, rather than on an author's reputation.	It is uncertain whether an article can ever truly be blind, especially in specialty niche areas. Reviewers can often identify the author through the article's style, subject matter, or self-citation.
Single blind review	Reviewer anonymity allows for impartial decisions free from influence by the author.	Reviewers may use their anonymity as justification for being unnecessarily critical or harsh when commenting on the author's work.
Open peer review	Some feel this is the best way to prevent malicious comments, stop plagiarism, prevent reviewers from drawing on their own agenda, and encourage open and honest reviewing.	Others argue that open peer review is a less honest process in which politeness or fear of retribution may cause a reviewer to withhold or tone down criticism. For example, junior reviewers may hesitate to criticize more esteemed authors for fear of damaging their career prospects.

The editor's role is to maintain and build the reputation of the journal. The editor of the high-ranking *Journal of Transport Geography* (Elsevier, 2013) identified these as his biggest challenges as editor:

- ❑ to maintain high academic standards through the peer-review process

- ❑ to establish and maintain a comprehensive, global network of transport geography contacts who can support the journal

- ❑ to encourage researchers, and especially early-years researchers, to submit their best research papers to the journal.

The other important concerns for journal editors are:

- ❑ to increase the impact factor (see Chapter 2) of the journal.

- ❑ to ensure that the journal is published (whether in print or online) on schedule.

All of this, of course, applies equally to all journals.

Being an editor involves many extra hours of work a year beyond the person's normal academic duties. For this reason, some journals have co-editors. In addition to their editorial duties, editors are also involved in teaching, researching, and writing at their respective institutions. Editors advise the publisher on the overall direction of the journal, appoint the members of the journal's editorial board, and manage submissions through the review process. Some editors are fortunate to have a part-time editorial assistant who helps them in their work, but many do not. Some publishers also provide dedicated administrative support to their editors, and others do not. If editors do not have this support, it means that they are performing all of the editorial duties on top of their other work.

Editors usually have a large number of submissions to deal with at any one time. The journal that Brian currently edits, for example, receives more than 400 submissions per year. That is more than one per day. Even though not all of these papers will go out for review, he still has to read them all to be able to make an initial decision on them. At the same time, he needs to follow the progress of other submissions that are currently being reviewed and make decisions on them when the reviews come in (see the Appendix for a flowchart of the peer review process).

Arranging reviews for articles is an enormous task that involves corresponding with reviewers, obtaining their feedback, and passing it on to authors. A key function of peer review is to help the editor determine an article's suitability for publication in the specific journal. The reviewers provide feedback and make recommendations, but it is the editor who makes the final decision as to what to tell the author. It is fairly common for reviewers to arrive at different decisions about a submission, so it is the editor who has to make a decision based on conflicting recommendations. Sometimes the editor will go with the recommendation made by the reviewer who has the most expertise in your topic; sometimes the editor may send the article out for another review in the attempt to get consensus among the reviews.

We aim to make the process of peer review transparent to new authors, especially so they have a better idea of what they can expect in this process. Brian, for example, has made this the topic of a number of editorials in the journal he currently edits by sharing the steps that are taken in reviewing submissions made to the journal so that prospective authors can better understand these processes and consider them as they prepare their manuscripts for submission. We have also, in our editorials, explained the criteria that are sent to reviewers when they are asked to review an article (Paltridge & Mahboob, 2014a). We have given advice to new authors for turning a dissertation into research articles (Paltridge & Mahboob, 2015) and, each year, have outlined research trends in terms of topics and methodologies that have underlaid articles that have been published in the journal (see, e.g., Paltridge & Mahboob, 2014b).

The editor also often reviews page proofs (sample pages of what the article will look like) for articles, answers queries from copyeditors (people who check the language of the article before it is published), and gives the final approval for articles to the publisher.

It is generally the editor who decides in which issue an article will appear, and there is often pressure from the publisher to meet deadlines that have been set for the publication of each issue. The process of determining what is in each issue, with some journals, has changed dramatically recently due to online publication. Now an issue "fills up" with articles as each one is received as corrected proofs and the article is assigned to a volume and given page numbers at the point at which it is officially ready for publication. In this instance, there is no need to wait for a full set of articles to be ready in order to publish an issue of the journal. This is referred to as article-based publishing.

The editor (or editors) also writes the editorial at the beginning of each issue—if the journal has one—to give an overview and frame the content of the papers in the issue for readers. With Sue's journal, once the publisher moved to article-based publishing, the editors decided not to write editorials because they no longer had control over which articles went in each issue.

A journal may also have themed or special issues, in which all the papers are on the same topic. Sometimes these special issues will be edited by the journal editor and, on other occasions, they are edited by guest editors. Even if the special issue is being handled by guest editors, the journal's main editor will still need to keep an oversight on the special issue and advise the guest editors on journal policies and review procedures, etc.

We have mentioned the various tasks and responsibilities of editors because you need to be aware of this when you are working with a journal editor, so that you do not have unrealistic expectations of what he or she will be able to do for you.

The Role of Reviewers in the Peer Review Process

Reviewers are typically university teachers and researchers who are specialists in the particular area of the journal. In the vast majority of cases, reviewers receive no monetary rewards for agreeing to

Our favorite authors are those that follow submissions requirements and guidelines to the letter and do not expect that the editor(s) will fix their submissions for them (see What Is Expected of You in the Peer Review Process (p. 78) for further discussion of this). On occasion, Brian has had to send back a submission to an author numerous times to get the references correct. He persisted until all the changes he asked for were made, mainly because an untidy reference list sends a bad impression to reviewers. A reviewer can think: "If the author has been this careless with the references, how much care has he or she put into the research on which the article is based? Maybe not a lot … ." This is not a message you want to send to reviewers.

review scholarly journal articles. Reviewing can be time consuming, sometimes requiring the equivalent of a day's work. Reviewers agree to review because they are interested in new work in their field and because they are committed to developing the field and its research. In addition, reviewing history has become a regular part of an academic's CV, so has implications for tenure and promotion.

Reviewers typically publish in the same journal that you are trying to be published in. It is the job of the reviewers to pay careful attention to the rigor of your study, your knowledge of the literature, the validity of the claims you make, and the contribution your study is making to the field. Despite stories you may hear about mean-spirited reviewers, most reviewers aim to provide helpful feedback that will improve the quality of your work. This will be discussed in the next section and in Chapter 5.

Once you become a published author, you will no doubt start receiving requests to review manuscripts. It is important to remember when you are reviewing that you should write the kind of review that you would like to receive—a review that is helpful and that shows a way forward to publication.

You should not assume that if an expert on your topic is on the editorial board for a journal that that person will necessarily be the reviewer for your article. While a condition of membership of an editorial board is that the person will agree to review a certain number of articles per year, it is not always the case that he or she is able to do this. He or she may be already reviewing an article when your submission comes in, so the editor will not ask the person to review another article at the same time. Or the reviewer may not be available to do reviews at that time for some other reason such as current work commitments, etc.

The Basic Peer Review Process

Regardless of the journal, the basic process of peer review is more or less the same. Once you have submitted an article to a journal, an editor reads it to decide if it has potential for publication in the particular journal. If he or she thinks that it does not (for example, it may be better suited to another journal), the editor will reject it in-house, sometimes called a *desk reject,* and notify you. Desk rejections are becoming increasingly common, with some journals making this decision for up to 80 percent of submissions (see "first review" questions on pages 73–74 for a discussion of criteria that might be used to make a desk reject decision).

We should stress that a desk reject does not necessarily mean your article is not publishable at all, so do not be discouraged by this. Read the reasons that are given to you by the editor for the rejection (if the editor has done this), take any advice you have been given, and then send your article to the next journal on your list of possible places for it to be published (or one that has been suggested by the editor if he or she has done this).

Some journal editors have a set of initial vetting questions they ask when they are looking at new submissions. If the answer is no to any of them, the article may be sent back for revision or it may be desk-rejected. This initial stage in the review process has become increasingly common over the past few years due to an increase in submissions to journals, which has, in some cases, doubled in recent years (Zuengler & Carroll, 2010), and which has led to more desk rejects than was the case in the past.

Common "first review" questions journal editors use to make a preliminary, in-house decision on an article include:

- ❑ Has the article been sent to the correct journal?
- ❑ Does the article report on original research?
- ❑ Has the author addressed the topic in a way that makes connections to the broader international readership of the journal?
- ❑ Does the article's Discussion section compare results of the study to previous research on the topic?
- ❑ Is it evident how the study moves the field forward?
- ❑ Are the sources referred to in the Literature Review and Discussion sections up to date?
- ❑ Is the article over the word length for submissions to the journal?
- ❑ Is the article under the word length for submissions to the journal?
- ❑ Has the article been prepared for blind review?
- ❑ Has the author used the correct referencing system for the journal?
- ❑ Can the author be identified from the acknowledgments?
- ❑ Are all figures and tables attached?

Editors regularly report that the most common reason for a desk rejection is that the article is not within the journal's aims and scope; that is, it has not been sent to the right journal. This point is related to the issue of targeting an appropriate journal that was discussed in

Chapter 2. Insufficient originality is another frequent reason an article may not be sent out for review. Beyond this, the most common reasons for rejection at this stage of the process, in our experience, are that the article does not report on research, it does not make connections to the international readership of the journal (see Chapter 2 for a discussion of this), and references are old or crucial sources on the topic have been omitted.

Thomson and Kamler (2013) list a number of other reasons that articles might be rejected at this stage. These include:

- ❑ The article is too informal or journalistic in style.
- ❑ The article may be a chapter from a dissertation and may not have been revised as a stand-alone journal article.
- ❑ The article may be a consultancy report and not be sufficiently located in the research literature for a submission to a peer-reviewed journal.
- ❑ The author hasn't consulted the notes for authors or has failed to follow the conventions of academic writing more generally.
- ❑ The article has been poorly presented and has not been proofread.
- ❑ The article is libelous, unethical, or rude.

If the editor decides to send your article out for review after successfully answering the first review questions, it will be sent to two, three, or even four reviewers.

The Criteria Reviewers Use to Assess Journal Articles

Most reputable journals provide guidelines and the criteria that reviewers use to assess articles. Be sure to read any reviewer or author guidelines provided on the website. Of course, not all reviewers will necessarily follow the criteria, but that information should still give you a good general idea of what reviewers are looking for.

Information on the peer review process and the criteria reviewers are asked to follow for journals published by the American Institute of Management Sciences (AIMS Press, n.d.) is given as an example.

AIMS Press

Peer Review Guidelines

All submissions to AIMS Press journals are subject to rigorous review. The standard peer review procedure is:

- ❑ All new submissions are reviewed by AIMS Press editors to ensure adherence to the requirements of AIMS Press journals, including English performance, scientific value, and ethical issues.

- ❑ Then the submission will be assigned one editor who will invite some external reviewers to review the submission further.

- ❑ Once the editors receive enough review reports, they will make the first decision on the manuscript: Accept, Revision, or Reject.

- ❑ The author of submission will receive the first decision and be asked to make the revision or submit the manuscript elsewhere.

- ❑ Upon resubmission, the Editor of AIMS Press journal will make the final decision on the manuscript: Accept, Further Revision, or Reject.

  www.aimspress.com/news/124.html

The criteria that Brian's current journal sends to reviewers is:

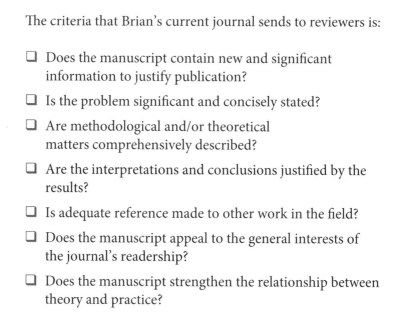

- ❏ Does the manuscript contain new and significant information to justify publication?

- ❏ Is the problem significant and concisely stated?

- ❏ Are methodological and/or theoretical matters comprehensively described?

- ❏ Are the interpretations and conclusions justified by the results?

- ❏ Is adequate reference made to other work in the field?

- ❏ Does the manuscript appeal to the general interests of the journal's readership?

- ❏ Does the manuscript strengthen the relationship between theory and practice?

These criteria show the importance of originality in the research on which the article is based, that the research has been well carried out, and that the claims made are justified by the data. They also highlight the importance of locating the article in the latest research and writing it up in a way that appeals to the broader field and in the specific area that is the focus of the research. The currency of the research is especially important.

Once your article has gone out to reviewers and they have commented on it, the editor will make a decision. Editors usually decide whether to *accept* your article, *accept it with minor revisions,* ask that you *revise and resubmit* your article, or *reject it.* The most common decisions, in our experience, are revise and resubmit and, unfortunately, reject. You will receive an email from the editor informing you of the decision and including all the reviewer comments. For minor revisions or revise and resubmit, you will need to consider and incorporate this feedback. More about responding to reviewer feedback is covered in Chapter 5.

If the decision you receive is anything other than reject, this is a good outcome and you can assume that the editor wants to publish your article.

How Long Does It Take to Be Reviewed?

The proliferation of journals and the increase in the number of articles being submitted to journals have led to a situation in which journal editors are finding it more difficult to find reviewers. In fact, one of the biggest issues editors talk about when they meet is how difficult it has become to find willing reviewers (Collins & Dagenais, 2010; Ellis, 2010) due to the multiple requests that good reviewers receive.

Sometimes we have had to ask as many 13 people to review an article before we have found someone who will agree to do it. Then we have to find another person to do it as well. Each article must have at least two reviewers. This requirement can draw out the review process time since we usually wait at least a week to hear back from a reviewer before we ask someone else to do it.

The most common reasons for a delay after deciding to send an article out for review are:

❑ finding suitable reviewers

❑ getting reviewers to agree to review

❑ ensuring reviewers submit the review by the due date

Even though many journals have automated reminder messages that go to reviewers when they are overdue, we often find we need to send a personal message to some reviewers to get the review. We could, of course, ask someone else to review the article when a review is not forthcoming, but this extends the review process even further so we are generally reluctant to do this. Further, because reviewers are busy people, they often ask for more time than was allocated to complete their review, and similarly, because finding good reviewers is such a challenge, we usually agree to this. Therefore, you may wait several months to get feedback on your article, something which is very often out of the control of the editor.

If the editor has decided to send your article out for review, you need to wait to hear back from the editor once the reviews are in for the decision on what happens next with your submission. You also need to be aware of how long it may take to get your article accepted for publication (much longer than most people realize). The time from submission to publication (if accepted) can also vary quite dramatically between journals, even among those in the same field of study. These time differences can be due to the number of articles that have already been accepted by the journal and are awaiting publication.

Another reason for the length of time it takes for an article to go through the review process is the amount of time reviewers are given to return their reports to the journal editor, which can range from one month to several months. Some journals now provide this information on their websites. For example, the journal *Global Environmental Change* has a link to what it calls *Speed Metrics,* journalinsights. elsevier.com/journals/0959-3780/speed, which shows the average number of weeks it takes for an article to be reviewed by the journal and the average number of weeks it takes for an article to reach key stages in the publication process. What you cannot do, however, is write to the editor and ask him or her to speed up the review process because you need to know the outcome of your submission for a job application (or promotion or tenure) purposes. Rather, you need to plan well ahead and allow plenty of time when you submit an article to a journal if this is one of your reasons for publishing. Your article may be finally accepted for publication, but this may be after several rounds of revisions. If each of your revisions is sent back to the reviewers for their comments, this can take some time.

Many journals now make it possible for an author to check the status of an article online while it is under review. For example, you can see which editor (if the journal has more than one) is handling your submission and when it was sent out for review. It is really important that you keep an eye on this.

What Is Expected of You in the Peer Review Process?

When you submit an article, all journals will have a number of expectations of you. The first is that the article you are submitting has not been submitted to another journal at the same time. This is called *dual* or *multiple submission* and is frowned upon in journal article publishing. This is nearly always stated in the author guidelines. Many journals will even ask you to sign a statement to this effect before they will proceed with your submission.

You should inform the journal editor if you wish to withdraw your submission from the journal or choose not to revise your article on

Several years ago, at the journal editors' meeting at a major conference, the editors of two leading journals in the field told a story. Each journal had received the same manuscript at the same time, and the editors discovered this because they had sent the manuscript to the same reviewer. Jointly, they wrote a very stern letter to the offending author, stating that he should not even think of submitting another manuscript to their journals at any time in the near future. They expected a profuse apology, but were surprised by the response. The author replied saying that he had never expected to be published in their prestigious journals, so hadn't thought he was doing anything wrong. What he really wanted was the helpful and thorough reviews so that he could revise his article and try to get it accepted at a less prestigious journal.

Although this author was correct in recognizing the very valuable feedback that reviews can provide for an article, he clearly did not realize the potential seriousness of what he had done. Editors consider this behavior to be unethical. Both journals will most likely not accept any future submissions from this author and, of course, the author will not receive any feedback from either journal. If, however, you do this and get through the review process with both journals, one of the journals is very likely to see your article in the other journal and will most likely retract your article—usually on its website in a very public manner—something which is not at all good for your academic career. And editors sometimes share names of people who do this with other editors as these situations arise. You don't want to be one of these names.

the basis of reviewers' comments. If you do not officially withdraw your article before submitting it elsewhere, it could be considered a double submission.

It is also important to respond to requests for revision promptly. Keeping in mind that many months have now passed since you finished your article and submitted it, if you wait too long, you may have to update your review of the literature and change the discussion of your findings in relation to research that has been published since you first wrote the article. Some journals give a deadline for returning the revised article; after that date they will consider it a new submission. Generally speaking, journals expect to receive revised articles within three months.

Throughout this whole process, you should respond to the editor promptly when he or she communicates with you, meet any deadline the editor sets, and be polite in all of your communications, even if you get a review decision you are not happy with.

If you have reproduced or adapted other people's work in your article, such as figures and tables, you will have to obtain permission to use this material from the original publisher of the material (not the author). It is a common mistake to think the author can grant you this permission. You may also have to obtain permission to use your own published work, although some publishers (such as Sage and Elsevier) do not require this. Provided your use is scholarly (as is the case with journal articles), most journal publishers will not require a fee for the use of already published material. Some, but not all, publishers, further, have opted out of permissions requests for the re-use of your own material, but you should check to see if this applies to you (see the International Association of Scientific, Technical & Media Publishers [www.stm-assoc.org/permissions-guidelines/] for more advice). You should also allow plenty of time for permissions requests since they can take a few weeks (or longer), and most publishers will not proceed with your article until you can show that you have been granted the required permissions.

How Long Should I Wait to Hear from the Journal after I Submit?

Because editors are dealing with a high volume of submissions at any one time, it is standard for authors to receive an automatic response that says that your article has been successfully uploaded into the system. At that point, you should be able to track the progress of your

> We are especially appreciative of "low maintenance" authors; that is, authors who follow the journal's submission guidelines and respond promptly to requests for information and revision. You want to be one of those people—someone the editor looks forward to hearing from and working with again.

article. If your article is out for review and you haven't heard back from the editor after three months, it is fine to email the editor directly and politely inquire about the status of your submission. This inquiry may encourage the editor to follow up more actively with the reviewers or, if the reviews are in, to make a decision about your submission.

An overview of the review process is presented in the Appendix.

What Happens after an Article Has Been Accepted?

Once an article has been accepted by a journal, there are still some changes you may be asked to make before it goes from the editor to the publisher. You may, for example, be asked to check that all your references follow the referencing style used by the journal. You will also be asked to make sure all your "author references" (if there are any) have been unblinded in the text and in the reference list; that is, you have placed the full reference(s) to your work back in the text. If you haven't yet sent the journal a bio (or bios), this is the time you should do this. Also, if you wish to add any acknowledgments to your article, this is the time to do it.

Once the article goes to the publisher it will be copyedited, in most cases by the publisher. After this you will be sent a copy of the proofs of your article to check and be asked to respond to any queries about missing references or any mismatches between your reference list and your text. You will not, however, be able to make other changes to your article at this stage. If new research on your topic has been published since you wrote your article, you will not, unfortunately, be able to add it. You must therefore make sure, then, before you sent off the final version of your article, that everything you want to include in your article is there at that time.

The length of time it takes for an article to appear in an issue of a journal varies from journal to journal, but most publishers now place accepted papers on their website in a section with a title such as Articles in Press or Early View so that people will know about your paper, even if it has not yet been assigned to an issue of a journal.

And, of course, you should celebrate and congratulate yourself for having had your article accepted for publication. This is a very exciting moment and tells you that all of the work you put into your article was worth it!

Chapter 5

Reading Reviewers' Reports and Addressing Their Concerns

As we noted in Chapter 4, after your article has gone through the first round of reviews, you will receive a letter from the editor with a decision and the reviewers' comments. The decision may be accept with minor revisions, revise and resubmit (sometimes called *major revisions*), or reject. While the first of these decisions is relatively easy to address, revise and resubmit and reject are the two categories that authors struggle with the most. How you respond to the reviewers' comments and what to do if you receive a rejection are topics that are discussed in this chapter.

Revise and Resubmit

Revise and resubmit is a common review outcome. In their book, *Writing for Scholarly Publication*, Casanave and Vandrick (2003, p. 261) emphasize that "revise and resubmit is not a rejection." But we know of doctoral students and early-career researchers who have misinterpreted the letter from the editor asking them to revise and resubmit as a rejection of their article. Revise and resubmit is an invitation to *revise* according to the reviewers' feedback and to *resubmit* to the same journal. A study of the publication histories of a series of articles submitted to an international Anglophone journal (Belcher, 2007, p. 1) suggested that a key factor leading to publication was

Brian has a friend who has published in many of the top journals in her field who, on receiving major revisions for her very first submission to a peer-reviewed journal, just put the article in her bottom drawer thinking the editor was not interested in her article and that this was effectively a rejection. When she told her supervisor this, he said, "Are you mad? This is good news. The editor wants your article. You just need to do more work on it!" She got the article out of the drawer, revised it, and sent it back to the journal, and it was published.

"authorial persistence"—the author's willingness to revise and resubmit the article through several rounds of revisions if necessary.

One of the key aims of peer review is to improve the quality of your paper, and most reviewers consider giving constructive feedback to be a key part of their role. Although it can sometimes be hard to accept the criticism as constructive, we believe that engaging in the peer review process will result in a better paper. One student described the experience of receiving reviewer feedback this way:

> Initially the amount of criticism was a shock. However, the process of addressing reviewers' concerns made it a much better paper and made me think about other issues that I hadn't previously considered. It was much more rigorous than any scrutiny the work had received before. It was a great learning process about what make a good paper. (Hartley & Betts, 2009, p. 41)

It is not uncommon to receive a letter from the editor similar to the letter from an editor received by a colleague of ours (see page 84). The letter opens with some good news for the author—the paper is "interesting," "well-written," and "relevant." Then the tone becomes negative, pointing out several weaknesses in the paper. The editor has carefully summarized what the author needs to do: engage more with the literature; clearly discuss the theoretical contribution, and, above all, show how the paper contributes to new knowledge. Research into journal article reviews (Belcher, 2007; Gosden, 2003) has found that the format used by this editor—some good news followed by the bad news—is commonly used by journal editors. To the first-time author, the number of things the editor requires may seem quite daunting, leading the author to abandon the task altogether. Again, the negative language used in this letter is not uncommon.

Letter from a Journal Editor

> Dear Dr. …
>
> As you will see, the reviewers found this to be an interesting and well-written paper focusing on an issue clearly relevant to the [Journal Name] readership. However, it was also generally agreed that the paper is deficient both in terms of a theoretical dimension and an analytical edge. Additionally, partly due to its insufficient engagement with established literature in this field, the paper fails to demonstrate convincingly how it adds to the existing sum of knowledge on this topic.
>
> Given the above comments, we regret that the paper in its present form cannot be accepted for publication in [Journal Name]. The editors would like to encourage you to consider submitting a substantially redrafted paper taking on board reviewers' observations (especially the numerous constructive suggestions by Reviewer 1). However, please note that resubmitting your manuscript does not guarantee eventual acceptance and that your resubmission will be subject to re-review before the editors reach a decision.
>
> We look forward to a resubmission.
>
> Yours sincerely,
> Editors

In a study that Brian carried out into how reviewers of journal articles learn to do peer review, one of the people he spoke to said, "I received many viciously worded reviews when I started publishing and decided that I would not be like them" (Paltridge, 2013, p. 11). Clearly, this reviewer had learned from her experience of being reviewed what not to do when writing a reviewer's report. Other things the reviewers said they found difficult were "being critical without being negative and unfair," "being supportive yet critical," and "saying no to an author gently." In all, though, the reviewers aimed to be constructive and supportive in the feedback they gave to authors even if, at times, they found it difficult to do this.

As Kwan (2010, p. 213) has pointed out, "Many first-time writers are confused, discouraged or even shocked by the negative reviews they receive and the substantial revisions requested . . . . Some never attempt to revise and resubmit their work that reviewers see as having potential for publication." The key message in this letter from the editor, however, is that the author is invited to revise and resubmit the paper. Our colleague, an experienced author, overcame his initial despondency at receiving this letter and revised the article in response to the detailed comments from three reviewers that were attached to the editor's email. The article has now been published. The other important point we would like to make is that even highly successful, well-published academics get negatively phrased feedback from editors and reviewers.

Responding to the Reviewers' Comments

If you have been invited to submit a revised version of your article, it is essential that once you have made the suggested changes, you write a response to the reviewers in which you provide a detailed account of all the changes you have made. It is important that you consider all comments made by the reviewers and not ignore the ones that you disagree with or that are too hard to respond to. Even if you are not going to modify your article in response to a specific criticism, you must give a reason why you have chosen not to amend your paper in response to it and be willing to accept the consequences of the decision.

Bear in mind that reviewers take the job of reviewing very seriously and may spend the equivalent of a full day reading and writing a report on your article. Based on her study of author responses to reviewers' reports, Feak (2009, p. 33) points out that "author responses are not arguments directed at proving the reviewers wrong. . . . they are more like polite discussions in which professionals can agree to disagree." She advises authors that they need to attend not only to the content revisions they have been asked to make but also to engage in a "polite" dialogue with the reviewers with whom they are interacting.

One of the first things we do as editors when a revised article is submitted is to look at the author's response to reviewers to assess whether the author has addressed *all* the reviewer recommendations and suggestions. Whenever you revise and resubmit an article, be sure to provide a detailed list of all the changes you have made. If there is no such list attached to the revised version, we will send a message to the author requesting one, which means another delay in a decision on your article.

Adopting a polite tone in your response is very important. Even if you are still feeling angry and upset by the comments, start by thanking the reviewers for their helpful feedback. It is a convention that is worth observing. The beginning of a response that Sue received from two authors who had been asked to make revisions to their article is an example of how to respond positively to reviewer feedback:

> Before itemizing our revisions, we'd like to thank the two reviewers who read over our previous revisions and commented on them so thoughtfully. The resulting changes, we believe, greatly enhance the manuscript. And thank you for giving us the opportunity to resubmit the manuscript for reconsideration.

Although there are different ways to respond to the reviewers' feedback, the author typically addresses each reviewer's comments separately. It is likely you will be dealing with an online system where there is a link for uploading your response to reviewers as a separate file when you upload your revised file. Before the advent of online systems, it was common to write a letter to the editor in which you listed all the changes you had made. These days, most authors simply upload a detailed list of the revisions they have made.

You will sometimes be given a date by which to submit the revised article. If you don't send it back by the due date, it will be considered a new submission and the whole review process will start again, so you do want to get it back by the date that the editor has set.

Table 5.1 contains an extract from a response we gave to reviewers' reports on an article we submitted to a journal. As the journal had a double blind peer review policy (see Chapter 4), the reviewers did not know who we were and we did not know who they were. Note how we begin by thanking the reviewers and then respond to each point, explaining what changes we have made to our article. Note also how we use the two-column format, which we think helps the reviewer and editor see exactly how we have responded because it is easy to compare our revisions with the reviewer's suggestion. As editors we also find this format very helpful.

Not all online systems, however, allow you to upload a table like this; they may have a text box into which you have to paste your response in a linear form. Brian's response to reviewer feedback on a paper submitted to a journal that had this requirement is shown in Table 5.2. He used a comment-response format with each reviewer comment followed by his response. Note how he also thanks the reviewers for their helpful comments.

Do not underestimate the amount of time needed to respond to reviewer feedback. Make sure your responses are appropriately detailed and clear. Indicate exactly what you have changed and where in the text you have made the changes. Including page numbers can be very helpful for the reviewer and the editor. Remember that your article is very likely to be sent back to the reviewers who recommended the revisions, and they will want to see how you have responded. You will help busy reviewers if you provide a detailed list of all your changes in your response so that they don't have to hunt through your article to try to find them. Editors don't just want to

Table 5.1

Extract from Sue and Brian's Response to Reviewers in Table Format

We thank the reviewers of their very helpful comments on our paper. Our responses to their comments are shown.

Response to Reviewer 1:

Reviewer's Comments	Our Response
1. p. 2. "as a high-stakes genre negotiates its way into the academy." Shouldn't this read "as a high-stakes genre in a non-traditional discipline negotiates its way into the academy" or something similar? It is not, after all, the genre per se that is the novel element.	A change has been made in accordance with the reviewer's suggestion.
2. p. 5. 'This is all' should be 'This all'.	This change has been made.
3. p. 6. How many supervisors were contacted for the survey? How were the supervisors and students that were interviewed selected, since it appears others could have been interviewed, too? What were the interviews about? How were the questions comprising what were presumably semi-structured interview schedules formed? And what did a typical interview schedule look like? Were the interviews text-based, drawing on potentially significant features the authors noticed from their analyses of the texts? There are no details of how interview data were coded and analyzed. Can a table that breaks down the different visual/performing arts areas of the theses be included?	We have reworked this section following the reviewer's feedback and have clarified the nature of the online survey as well as provided information on interview participant selection and interview themes (as well as providing schedules in Appendix 1). We also clarify the role the written texts played in the interviews and provide details of interview data and analysis. Table 1 now provides a breakdown of the 36 theses into areas of study.

===== **Table 5.2** =====

Extract from Brian's Response to Reviewers in Linear Format

I would like to thank the reviewers for their helpful comments on my work. I have addressed each of the issues raised by the reviewers in my revised submission. The reviewers' comments and my responses to their comments are listed below.

Reviewer's Comment

p. 5 "There were 104 submissions to the journal in the year that the data were collected." Unless there are some proprietary or other reasons not to do so, it would be useful to state the actual year in which the data was collected.

Brian's Response

When asked to participate in the study one of the reviewers asked that all possible identifying information be removed from the reviews and that the data not be used or reported on in a way in which he could possibly be identified. For this reason, the year that the data were collected has not been included in the text. I have also not quoted from his reports in this paper. (All the other reviewers agreed for quotes from their reports and the questionnaires they completed to be included in publications.)

see brief comments like "I have made the changes." They want a clear description of what has changed and to see the revised text in your list of changes. Doing this will ensure that you don't receive this sort of feedback on your revised version:

> Although some of my comments have been incorporated, there is still a serious weakness in the results and possibly their presentation. Because the authors have not given a point-by point response to the initial reviews, it is not possible to know why some comments were responded to and others not. (from an anonymous reviewer)

On the other hand, there is probably no need to write a page of commentary in response to a one-sentence comment by a reviewer. If it seems to you that the reviewer has not understood a point you are making, read through the section carefully and ask yourself how clear it really is. As Feak (2009) notes, if all reviewers have made the same comment about your research, it is not necessary to respond to this three times; simply acknowledge that this is a common response and indicate once how you have dealt with it. Sometimes one reviewer comments negatively on a feature of your article but the other reviewer is more positive. You can note this, but you should try to show that you understand what the negative comments are saying. You don't, of course, have to comply with everything the reviewers say, but if you do disagree with them, do so in a way that maintains politeness conventions and provides a clear set of reasons as to why you would like to retain your original position rather than simply stating "I disagree."

Table 5.3 shows authors' responses to reviewer recommendations from a study by Feak (2009, p. 28). In each case, the authors are disagreeing with the reviewer's comment, but some responses appear to be more "polite" than others. The first three responses are fairly blunt; the second response verges on rudeness, and the fourth response can be seen to be violating implicit politeness conventions as it portrays the reviewer in a negative light through its use of *obviously*. Feak (2009) (p. 28) points out that the final response has a rather different tone and can be seen as a more polite disagreement because it "begins by agreeing with the reviewer and acknowledging the value of the suggestion." The author's use of *however* indicates that he or she may not comply fully with the reviewer's recommendation, but the author does offer to carry out a smaller scale revision to accommodate the reviewer's suggestion.

It is also worth noting how in Author response (4), the author is able to refer to Reviewer 2's comment that the paper should be shorter to argue against the expanded discussion that Reviewer 1 is recommending. This can sometimes be a helpful strategy when the reviewers are asking for contradictory changes. The author does, however, agree to add a reference, so does not totally ignore Reviewer 1's suggestion.

When revising your article in response to reviewer feedback, be careful not to go too far over the journal's word length. Responding to the reviewers' comments does usually mean your article will increase in length. Editors expect you to manage to respond while not going too far over the maximum length. We usually ask authors to not add

Table 5.3

Author Responses to Reviewers That Disagree with the Recommendation

Reviewer Comment	Author Response
1. Further details of the surgical procedure should be provided.	1. The reviewer is welcome to come and observe the procedure at our institute.
2. VATS lobectomy does not necessarily offer better pulmonary function.	2. We disagree.
3. I would suggest some further discussion on the benefits of VATS.	3. The advantages of VATS have been very well documented elsewhere. Such a discussion would add to the length of the paper, which Reviewer 2 has suggested reducing. We have added one reference that explores the advantages, but have not changed the text otherwise.
4. I do not see how the authors can conclude from the data that posterolateral thoracotomy should be avoided. Studies have shown that the procedure does not result in a greater number of post-operative complications.	4. The reviewer has obviously misunderstood our point here. We do in fact state that there were no significant differences in the posterolateral thoracotomy group and the VATS group. We do, however, believe that overall VATS is a better procedure.
5. A cost-benefit discussion would enhance the paper considerably.	5. We agree that a discussion of cost-benefit would indeed be informative. Such information would allow others to better evaluate the benefits of the new procedure. However, such a discussion would really need to be undertaken in a separate paper given the scope of the issue. For our purposes here, then, we have added an algorithm that roughly provides a sense of the costs.

more than 1,000 words. It did happen to Sue, however, that on a few occasions, right before the final acceptance of an article, she noticed that the article had somehow grown from 8,000 to 13,000 words. At that late stage, she then had to ask the author to cut back. In the age of electronic journals, you may ask why a 13,000-word article is a problem. From our perspective it's an equity issue: it's simply not fair to other authors who have adhered to the word limit to communicate their research findings.

Brian once submitted an article to *Studies in Higher Education* (published as Paltridge, 2015a) in which he examined how reviewers asked for changes to be made to submissions to peer-reviewed journals. A lot of these requests, it seemed to him, were made indirectly as suggestions or recommendations, rather than as directions. To explore this question, he examined a set of reviewers' reports from the point of view of speech act theory, a theory that examines how people work out what other people mean by what they say (which is often somewhat different from the literal meaning of what they say). This seemed to him to be a fairly suitable theory to explore his question, and in his data analysis section, he simply said that "a speech act analysis was carried out on the recommendations that reviewers made for changes to the submissions" and then explained the history and concerns of speech act theory. One of the reviewers, however, said that "there is no explanation of the process used for the speech act analysis." To address this comment, Brian explained how he had carried out his analysis. He added: "These recommendations were then classified in terms of kinds of speech act (such as a direction or suggestion), whether they were direct or indirect, and the relation between the occurrence of these speech acts and the category of recommendation made by the reviewer." To a reader in the area of linguistics, or this case, pragmatics, this explanation may have been unnecessary, but for readers in the area of higher education it clearly was needed as they would not have known, at all, how he would have done his analysis.

It may be possible to place some of the content from your article, particularly data-related content, into the online Supplementary Material section that most electronic journals now have. As editors, we would advise authors to do this where possible in order not to lengthen their article too much. You can put data, video, audio, and other relevant materials into Supplementary Materials that are accessed via a link in your article.

Understanding What Reviewers Are Asking You to Do

Sometimes reviewers are quite clear as to what they expect the author to do. For example, this comment explicitly tells the author to revise the introduction:

> The paper requires a proper and concise introduction. At present the introduction extends over 6 pages and is, in fact, a very detailed and overly lengthy account of [the topic]. What is required is a short (500–1,000 words) introduction that sets out the key issues, the structure and methodology of the paper, and its key arguments.

Authors often have difficulty understanding, or decoding, what exactly reviewers want them to do (Feak, 2009; Fortanet, 2008; Paltridge, 2015a; Thomson & Kamler, 2013). Generally, the rules of politeness prevail, with reviewers seeming quite reluctant to directly instruct or order authors to make changes to their manuscripts, making it particularly difficult for new researchers to understand exactly which things they must do and which are optional. Paltridge (2015a, p. 112) provides a few reviewer suggestions that an inexperienced author might not interpret as instructions to make a correction even though they are:

- ❏ "Below are some references to intercultural communication I suggest you familiarize yourself with."
- ❏ "It would be worth citing a more recent volume."

As stated earlier, reviewer recommendations are often couched in indirect language, making them quite tricky to interpret. For example, the comment, "the author provides no conclusion" (Paltridge, 2015a) is not a simple statement of fact but is intended to ask the author to add a conclusion. Similarly, the use of the phrase *I suggest* in the sentence "I suggest that the claim be removed unless it can be warranted by more convincing data" is not a helpful suggestion by the reviewer but a directive to either provide more data or to remove the claim (Paltridge, 2015a).

Since all academic articles are making claims based on the research, the writer hopes that his or her peers (the reviewers and then the readers) will accept those claims and, in essence, validate the research. Authors have to be careful not to make claims that are too strong or too weak; they must be able to justify them in terms of the evidence provided (see Chapter 3). It is quite common for reviewers to comment on this aspect of articles they are reviewing with comments such as, "The claim that the task is too great is an assertion but not supported. More reasons need to be given."

Feak (2009) points out that authors struggle to interpret reviewer comments that take the form of questions. Is the reviewer directing the author to make a change, or is the reviewer merely posing a question or making a suggestion that the author can choose to respond to or choose to ignore? If a reviewer says, "Are you saying that bilinguals are naturally more creative than monolinguals?" the reviewer most likely wants the author to clarify something said in the article; the reviewer is not just asking a question (Paltridge, 2015a, p. 112).

We have inserted comments into Table 5.4, an extract of a response to reviewers on an article that we wrote, to highlight what we think the reviewers were really asking us to do. Their comments read for the most part like polite suggestions or requests. In fact, if you look at our responses in the second column, you can see that we understood the reviewers to be asking us to make changes. It seemed to us that the reviewers were commenting on the extent of the claims we were making for our study and, on four occasions, we responded by saying that we had modified the extent of our claims.

When Brian first attempted publication in peer-reviewed journals, he would ask a colleague to open the editor's letter (in those days it was a letter) and read the reports to him. They would then have a long discussion about what he should do with his paper in response to the reports. Now that he is a much more experienced writer, he deals with reviewers' reports much more systematically and methodically. And he has learned how to interpret a reviewer's report and what comments such as "It might be an idea to …" and "I would suggest …" really mean. He has learned, in particular, that in a reviewer's report a suggestion is very rarely just a suggestion. More commonly, it is a directive to make a change to the submission.

Note that Reviewer 2 asks several questions about the implications of our study. First, the reviewer tells us to be more specific and then asks about a study we cited. We interpreted these questions as directives, not requests for clarification, but rather than provide the information requested, we realized that this theme was not central to our arguments and deleted this part of the discussion. However, the final question, "What is learnt from their experiences?" was understood by us to be a requirement to provide more information, to which we responded to by saying, "We suggest ways in which our study could assist teachers of advanced academic writing and thesis supervisors in the visual and performing arts."

A study by Feak (2009) identified a number of commonly used verbs that authors use when responding to reviewers' feedback. Often these are used in the past tense (*I changed . . .*) or the present perfect (*I have changed . . .*) as authors explain what they have done to revise the paper. These verbs have a range of meanings, as shown in Table 5.5, and could be useful when writing responses to reviewers. You may also want to look at the verbs we used in the responses to our reviewers in Table 5.4.

Table 5.4

A Response to Reviewers' Reports with Our Comments

Response to Reviewers' Comments

We thank the reviewers for their helpful comments. Our responses are shown.

Reviewer 1

Is this a recommendation or an instruction?

Reviewer Comment	Our Response
A well written and presented article, which has something to contribute. My main recommendations have to do with adding a broader contextualisation and toning down, at least a little, some of the claims made.	We have provided a broader contextualisation while attempting to remain within word limit. We have narrowed the scope of our claims. *We recognise that this is an instruction to modify some of our claims.*
The reviewer politely disagrees with some of our claims. I think some of your comments minimise the variation that exists within the doctorate between and within other fields, and between countries. Even leaving aside the recent distinction between professional and conventional doctorates, there are considerable variations within the conventional doctorate (e.g., length of thesis, thesis as a whole or a series of articles, submission of published work, use of first person, inclusion of non-textual material) and its examination (e.g., number of examiners, public or private examination), showing how its form has been able to accommodate many different needs.	We have recognised this in our revised text. *We acknowledge that this is an instruction and make revisions.*
This is an indirect instruction to modify our claims. If you looked at professional doctorates in particular areas—e.g., education, business/management, engineering—you would probably find analogous tensions to those you describe (on p. 26) between the artist and the researcher, but in this case between the practitioner/professional and the researcher.	*We understand the reviewer is pointing out a problem in our argument. We decide to remove this point rather than defend our position.* We have removed reference to these tensions.
The reviewer makes a polite suggestion: "be more cautious." I'd also be a bit more cautious in talking about the history of doctorates in the performing arts, unless you have thoroughly checked the sources.	*We interpret the suggestion as an instruction and again modify our claims.* Overall, we have tempered our claims that we have made when talking about the history of doctorates in the performing and visual arts. Our point about there being no well-established tradition is clarified below.
Reviewer asks us a direct question. p. 26, 22 Are you going to compare Macleod's and Elkins' typologies?	We have now done this. *We interpret it as a direct instruction to compare the typologies.*
Reviewer makes a statement. p. 27, 37 Though in practice "the options and choices available" may be limited by the "traditions" developed in the particular institutions/departments concerned.	We acknowledge the limitations of the local on choice in the conclusion and draw on our interview data to suggest how options and choices are shaped by institutional and individual forces. *We interpret it as an instruction to qualify the claims we are making.*

Table 5.4 (continued)

A Response to Reviewers' Reports with Our Comments

Reviewer 2

Reviewer Comment	Our Response
Positioning of the paper in the literature. This is well argued and the significance of this paper is established.	We have modified the scope of our initial claims.

Polite suggestion from reviewer. [pointing to the first comment]

Again we understand we have overstated our claim and modify it. [pointing to "We have modified the scope of our initial claims."]

Reviewer Comment	Our Response
Perhaps the final sentence of the introduction could be less ambitious. This paper can contribute to filling the gap. The diversity of presentation of doctoral theses in this discipline suggests further research will be needed rather than having the gap filled by this paper.	

Reviewer Comment	Our Response
It would help the reader to have clearer signposting, to distinguish this paper from the bigger study that is mentioned. This signposting can occur early in the paper and along the way. For example, on page 7 the paragraph begins "The data that was drawn on for the study...." It sounds like all the data from both stages will be drawn on for this paper. Another example, the findings section jumps straight into findings about the texts yet the reader has just read that there are multiple sources of data e.g. supervisor survey, interviews, etc. An introduction would alert the reader to the sources of data analysed for presentation in this section and the key contribution to theory and practice that emerged from this data analysis. The substance for analysis in this paper is two theses yet it is page 10 before the reader finds this out.	We have attempted to provide clearer signposting for the reader to distinguish the larger study from the focus of this article which we introduce on p. 7. We have provided information on the data we draw on for our analyses of the 2 theses.

"It would help the reader .." might seem like a polite suggestion. [pointing to the second comment]

We interpret it as a direct instruction to provide clearer signposting.

Reviewer Comment	Our Response
Implications Be more specific about what the examination of the nature and character of the two doctoral texts adds beyond being 'richly individual'. For example: Did the two students interviewed have experiences similar to, or different from, those reported by Hockey and Allen-Collinson (2005)? Did the two students experience 'identity struggles'? What is learnt from their experiences?	We have removed the later references to Hockey and Allen-Collinson and to identity struggles as they were not the prime focus of this paper. We suggest ways in which our study could assist teachers of advanced academic writing and thesis supervisors in the visual and performing arts.

The reviewer asks two direct questions.

We respond to this direct request and provide further information.

Table 5.5

Verbs That Are Commonly Used to Respond to Reviewers

Verbs Linked to Writing and General Revision Activities	Verbs That Show an Addition	Verbs That Show a Reduction	Verbs That Clarify
address	add	shorten	explain
alter	include/now	omit	specify
change	includes	remove	define
modify	now listed	delete	describe
revise		reduce	simplify
rewrite			compare
rephrase			discuss
rework			better identify
			further elaborate
			detail
			correct

Source: Adapted from Feak, 2009.

Deciding Not to Revise

Of course, it may be that after studying the reviewers' reports, you decide that the amount or type of revision demanded is simply not possible for you to carry out. This recently happened to us when, after one round of revisions, our article came back to us with one of the reviewers asking questions that we felt we would be unable to respond to. We decided to withdraw our article and submit it elsewhere. The ending was a happy one! It got published (after further revisions) in the second journal to which we submitted. So, if you ultimately feel that you will not be able to satisfy the reviewers' expectations, consider withdrawing and resubmitting elsewhere. If you do this, try to incorporate as many of the requests for changes as you can and then, before submitting elsewhere, make sure to follow the guidelines for authors set by that journal (including the word length and referencing style required by the journal).

Dealing with a Rejection

Most scholars will have experienced rejection at least once in their career and probably more times than that. What distinguishes a successful academic from a less successful one is that the successful one has survived that initial rejection and has absorbed the reviewers' and editor's feedback, has revised the paper, and has submitted it elsewhere—sometimes to several journals (one at a time)—before finding a "home" for it.

When Ryuko Kubota, now a well-published professor at a Canadian university, was in the earlier stages of her academic career, she offered this advice to beginning scholars: "Never give up. If one journal rejects your paper, it does not necessarily mean that your manuscript is not worth publishing. If you think your manuscript presents legitimate arguments, send it to another journal" (Kubota, 2003, p. 68).

Of course, as we pointed out in Chapter 4, there are two distinct types of rejection that an author can experience. The first is the in-house or desk rejection where the article is rejected without being sent out for review. The second type of rejection occurs after your article has been reviewed and the reviewers' recommendation to the editor is that your article is not suitable for publication in the journal. In this case, you will typically receive at least two fairly detailed sets of feedback. Now your article has the benefit of feedback from two experts in your field and possibly some additional comments by the editor. You need to give all of these comments serious consideration and use this feedback to improve your article.

A decision by the editor not to take your submission further is something that all academics have dealt with in their careers. Because one's initial response is often despair or anger, or a mixture of both, it is very important not to fire off a hasty, angry response to the editor. Johnson (2011) recounts that she once received an outright rejection on a Saturday morning, and, feeling upset and angry, spent the rest of the day revising it in terms of the feedback. By 5:00 PM, she had submitted it to another journal. When the resubmitted article was rejected by the new journal, she realized that she had not spent enough time understanding what the reviewers were asking and therefore had not given enough thought to choosing a more appropriate journal.

The best advice we can give is to read the reviews and then set them aside and look at them a few days later. As you read them, Johnson (2011) recommends asking yourself:

❑ Are they reasonable according to the journal's guidelines?

❑ Have I actually understood what the reviewers are saying?

❑ Can I clearly articulate why the reviewers are recommending rejection?

Remember that the reviewers are likely to be people whose work you have cited and experts in your field. Their comments are worth paying attention to. Although you may find it hard to show the reports to someone else, it is probably a good idea to ask a colleague or your advisor to give you an opinion of the reviews. There could be many reasons for the non-acceptance of your article by a particular journal, and it's important to spend time making sure you understand why your article is not considered suitable.

Avoid writing an angry letter or email to the editor complaining about the decision or the quality of the reviews before you have had time to let the feedback sink in. If, after serious consideration, you believe that you have genuine grounds for contesting the quality of the reviews, then write a polite, well-reasoned letter to the editor that sets out your case.

Li (2006) recounts the experience of one PhD student in Physics who successfully appealed the decision to not accept his article for publication by the journal *Physical Review Letters*. The student had initially submitted the article to *Science*, a highly regarded journal, where it was rejected and not sent out for review. He then revised it in consultation with his supervisors and submitted it to *Physical Review Letters*, a more specialized journal. After two rounds of revisions and five reviewers' reports, the editor made the following decision: "Although comments on the scientific content were generally favourable, the suitability for *Physical Review Letters* has been questioned. We consider the latter argument [by the reviewer] persuasive and cannot accept the paper for publication" (Li, 2006, p. 471).

The student then wrote an appeal letter, as allowed by the journal's official appeal procedures, arguing why his article should not be rejected. Two months later, he received a favorable letter from the editor stating that the associate editor who had reviewed his article recommended that it be accepted for publication after all. Not all journals may have the same formalized appeals process, but it is worth looking on the journal's website to see whether such a procedure does exist. Alternatively, a polite letter to the editor may be worth considering if you really feel you have strong grounds for appealing the decision. In this student's case, several of the reviews were quite positive and, as the editor noted, comments on the science were "generally" positive, encouraging the student to write his appeal letter.

It's hard to know how frequently authors successfully appeal a rejection. We believe editors try to behave fairly, so if you can provide evidence that your work was not given fair consideration, you may be successful. If you get to a point where you are thinking of appealing a decision to reject your paper, we advise you to first discuss this with your advisor or with your colleagues to make sure it is the best course of action for you.

Sometimes, however, after investing a lot of time and effort revising your paper based on the reviewers' feedback, and after resubmitting it to the same journal, you may receive a letter like the one shown. The advice given earlier applies in this case too: Carefully consider the feedback, seek advice, don't do anything that you might regret, and consider submitting to another journal once you've revised taking the reviewers' comments into account.

Dear _____,

Thank you for resubmitting your paper to [journal]. We have now received external referees' reports, and these are included at the end of this email for information.

As you will see, there is agreement among the reviewers that the paper has improved since its first submission. Unfortunately, the balance of opinion among second round reviewers' recommendations clearly lead the editors to reject the paper for publication.

I am sorry to convey this disappointing news, but as editors we hope that the additional comments provided by reviewers, particularly Referee One, will assist you in improving the paper further should you decide to submit to another journal.

Yours sincerely,
Editor

English Proficiency and the Review Process

As we have previously advised, when deciding which journal to submit your article to, it is very important to consult the journal's instructions to authors. However, as Gosden (2003) has pointed out, specific guidance for authors who do not speak English as their first language is rare. There are numerous reports of authors having their manuscripts returned with comments such as "have this edited by a native English speaker" (e.g., Belcher, 2007; Lillis & Curry, 2010). So, to what extent do authors who are not native speakers get rejected on the basis of their English language proficiency? While these studies point out the difficulties that non–English speaking scholars experience when trying to publish in English language journals, what is less clear is how these difficulties differ from those experienced by native English speakers. Given that most top-tier journals have high rejection rates, many authors, regardless of their language background, struggle to get published.

In this next section, we briefly consider the role of English language proficiency in reviewer feedback and suggest some ways in which authors who are concerned about their English could work on their articles prior to submission. Many of our suggestions apply regardless of proficiency in English.

Reviewers of articles by non-native speakers of English submitted to English language journals have been found to comment on both the scientific content and the written language of the articles (e.g., Belcher, 2007; Bocanegra-Valle, 2015). Mungra and Webber's (2010) study of 33 reviewers' comments identified that more than half the reviewer comments (56 percent) were based on the content of the articles and only about 44 percent were based on language. These were research articles submitted to international English language medico-scientific journals and written by researchers who do not speak English as a first language who work in an Italian medical school. The most common comments on the content of the articles would apply equally to all articles:

- ❏ an incomplete literature
- ❏ a lack of association between claim and data
- ❏ a lack of procedural rigour
- ❏ a lack of explanation of why data were unusual
- ❏ scientific reasoning errors in the researcher's own data (Mungra & Webber, 2010)

The most frequent comments about language use were "not well written" and "lack of clarity," which are obviously vague and unhelpful (Mungra & Webber, 2010). There were also more specific comments like "non-standard English is used throughout the manuscript … so much so that it prevents, at times, the manuscript from being comprehensible" (p. 49) and "also it would be clearer if the sentence advantages over [technical detail] were broken up into two sentences" (p. 49). Although the first comment is about non-standard English, the second one might apply to any author, regardless of language background. Similarly, comments that relate to how strongly an author makes a claim for the findings are not necessarily related to the language status of the writer.

In Belcher's (2007) study of reviewer comments on the work of native and non-native speakers of English from developing countries who submitted articles to an international peer-reviewed journal, comments on what she called the "vague category" of language use/style were more frequent than any other features she studied but common to all reviews. Belcher argues that factors such as knowledge of relevant topics, relevant research literature and research methods, genre conventions, audience expectations, and access to resources that facilitate research and publication may in fact play a more important role in getting published than language proficiency.

Gosden's (1992) survey of 116 native–English speaking editors of leading science journals identified the four language-related aspects most likely to influence their judgment of the merits and acceptability of submissions by non-native English speakers. Although carried out in the 1990s, the findings are still pertinent. The four aspects the editors identify as potentially troublesome—other than grammatically incorrect sentences—are not specifically restricted to non-native speakers of English:

- ❏ logical and clear linking of sentences for the reader
- ❏ development of the topic from sentence to sentence in a coherent way
- ❏ use of grammatically correct sentences
- ❏ ability to skillfully use the language needed when making claims.

More recent research suggests that attitudes toward the strict application of rules of English grammar may be shifting, particularly in fields where the majority of authors are not native English language speakers. Rozycki and Johnson (2013) studied 14 published articles that had been awarded Best Paper in the *IEEE Transactions* (a series of prestigious engineering journals) in the fields of software and hardware engineering and identified numerous instances of what they called non-canonical English grammar. (Non-canonical grammar refers to language considered unacceptable or non-standard according to *A Comprehensive Grammar of the English Language* by Quirk et al., 1985.) Examples of non-canonical grammar are missing/incorrect articles, lack of subject-verb agreement, verbs in place of nouns, and misuse of prepositions. It may be that this development is particular to fields like engineering, so it should be treated with caution by those who are working in other fields of study. Interestingly, the only paper of the 14 to be free of any non-canonical grammar was a single-authored paper written by a non-native speaker of English.

It is nevertheless clearly in the author's interest to submit a paper that is free of language-based errors because this will make it easier for the reviewer to follow the content and the arguments the author is making. Poorly written papers are unlikely to pass the initial in-house review stage.

In Chapter 1, we introduced the idea of literacy brokers: friends, advisors, colleagues, editors, reviewers, or proofreaders who provide advice to academic writers and who can be very helpful if you want to improve the quality of your academic writing. Ryuko Kubota (2003), whose first language is Japanese but who has published many articles in English, has this advice for non-native English speakers who are writing for publication in English language journals: "Try to find a good copyeditor who not only has good linguistic skills but also the ability to retain your original intentions" (p. 68).

Other helpful suggestions include:

- ❏ drawing on the help of academic peers (fellow students, colleagues) and English-speaking friends wherever they are in the world

- ❏ sharing drafts and seeking feedback prior to submission

- ❏ joining a writing group where you not only get feedback on your work but also practice giving feedback to other writers.

If you have sought help from a language editor in preparing your article, it may be helpful to ask this person to also look at your response to the reviewers. It is essential that the reviewers and the journal editor understand how you are responding but also recognize that your response is appropriately polite even when you may be disagreeing with a specific comment. This is a delicate balance that requires skilful use of language.

Where To Go from Here?

So, where do you go from here? If you've not yet started, get publishing! And keep at it. This is important for you now and in your future career. Start with your best idea or piece of work. Choose a journal you think is the best, follow our advice, and submit it. Take the reviewers' comments seriously, even if they have a different point of view from yours, and consider their feedback as your rework your article. Don't be discouraged by what might seem a lot of revision. For most articles, this is the norm and doesn't necessarily mean that your article is not publishable.

In a chapter titled "Getting Published and Doing Research," Guofang Li (2012, p. 161), who moved from China to Canada in the mid-1990s to earn her PhD and is now a faculty member at Michigan State University, gives this advice to beginning academic authors: "Write, write, write!"

We couldn't agree more. Plan your writing, put aside time for writing, and write.

Appendix: Flowchart of the Peer Review Process

Submission (usually electronic) is made through the journal's website.

↓

A quick review by the editor determines whether the paper is suitable for the journal.

↓

Possible desk rejection; the editor sends it back to the author for changes; <u>or</u> the editor selects 2–3 reviewers who are considered to be knowledgeable on the subject investigated and invites them to review (see Basic Peer Review Process, Chapter 4, for more details on this).

↓

The editor or assistant monitors the time allotted for review taken; reminders are sent if necessary or an alternate reviewer is sought if a review does not come in.

↓

Reviewers complete their evaluation of the submission and provide recommendations for the author(s) and the editor.

↓

The editor makes a decision whether to accept, ask for revisions, or reject the submission and informs the author by email.

↓

If revisions are required (the most common outcome), the author revises, addressing the issues raised by the reviewers.

↓

The author prepares a response to the reviewers that makes it clear which changes have been made to the submission based on the reviewers' comments (see Responding to Reviewers' Comments, Chapter 5).

↓

The paper is re-reviewed by the editor and at least one of the original reviewers, or new reviewer(s) are invited, depending on the extent of the revisions.

↓

Reviewers send in reports recommending acceptance/ further revisions/ rejection/ of the submission.

↓

The editor makes a decision whether to accept, ask for revisions, or reject the submission and informs the author by email.

↓

If the article is accepted, it moves in to the production process.

REFERENCES

Ahmad, U.K. (1997). Research article introductions in Malay: Rhetoric in an emerging research community. In A. Duszak (Ed.)., *Culture and styles of academic discourse* (pp. 273–304). New York: Mouton de Gruyter.

AIMS Press. (n.d.). *Peer review guidelines.* Available at http://www.aimspress.com/news/124.html

American Psychological Association. (2010). *Publication manual of the American Psychological Association* (6th ed.). Washington, DC: American Psychological Association.

Anyangwe, E. (2012). *Getting it write: Best practice in academic writing.* Available at http://www.guardian.co.uk/higher-education-network/blog/2012/jul/25/the-art-of-academic-writing

BAAL. (1993). Forum: Getting published in academic journals. *British Association for Applied Linguistics Newsletter, 43,* 9–15.

Beall, J. (n.d.). *Scholarly open access. Critical analysis of scholarly open-access publishing.* Available at scholarlyoa.com/individual-journals

Belcher, D. D. (2007). Seeking acceptance in an English-only research world. *Journal of Second Language Writing, 16,* 1–22.

Belcher, W. L. (2009). *Writing your journal article in 12 weeks: A guide to academic publishing success.* Los Angeles: Sage.

Bell, J., & Waters, S. (2014). *Doing your research project: A guide for first time researchers* (6th ed.). Maidenhead, U.K.: McGraw-Hill.

Bocanegra-Valle, A. (2015). Peer reviewers. Recommendations for language improvement in research writing. In R. P. Alastrué & C. Pérez-Llantada (Eds.), *English as a scientific and research language* (pp. 207–230). Berlin: Walter de Gruyter.

Brown, R. (1994). Write right first time. *Literati Newsline,* Special Issue for Authors and Editors, 1994/1995. Available at http://web.archive.org/web/19971014014626/http://www.mcb.co.uk/literati/write.htm

Cambridge University Press. (2015). Cambridge Journals. Available at http://journals.cambridge.org/action/stream?pageId=2488&sessionId=C68CA35EC6F45A5646355AD21FEA0371.journals

Canadian Journal of Communication. (n.d.). Index. Available at www.cjc-online.ca/index.php/journal

Carnell, E., MacDonald, J., McCallum, B., & Scott, M. (2008). *Passion and politics: Academics reflect on writing for publication*. London: Institute of Education, University of London.

Casanave, C. P. (2009). Writing up your research. In J. Heigham & R.A. Croker (Eds.), *Qualitative research in applied linguistics* (pp. 288–305). New York: Palgrave Macmillan.

Casanave, C. P., & Vandrick, S. (Eds.). (2003). *Writing for scholarly publication: Behind the scenes in language education*. Mahwah, NJ: Lawrence Erlbaum.

Colic-Peisker, V. (2012, 5 August). Beware the scammers targeting academics. *The Australian*, 17.

Collins, L., & Dagenais, D. (2010). Perspectives from the *Canadian Modern Languages Review/ La revue canadienne des langues vivantes*: Comments from the co-editors. *The Modern Language Journal, 94*, 638–640.

Day, A. (2007). *How to get research published in journals* (2nd ed.). Aldershot, U.K.: Gower.

Department of Industry, Innovation, Science, Research and Tertiary Education. (2012). *Higher education research data collection: Specification for the collection of 2011 data*. Canberra: Department of Industry, Innovation, Science, Research and Tertiary Education, Australian Government.

Ellis, R. (2010). Policy and procedure in journal editing. *The Modern Language Journal, 94*, 654–657.

Elsevier. (2013). Editor in the spotlight—Richard Knowles. Available at editorsupdate.elsevier.com/2013/03/editor-in-the-spotlight-richard-knowles/

Elsevier. (2015a). At a glance. Available at www.elsevier.com/about/at-a-glance

Elsevier. (2015b). Peer review. Available at www.elsevier.com/reviewers/peer-review

Feak, C. B. (2009). Negotiating publication: Author responses to peer review of medical research articles in thoracic surgery. *Revista Canaria de Estudios Ingleses, 59*, 17–34.

Feak, C. B., & Swales, J. M. (2011). *Creating contexts: Writing introductions across genres*. Ann Arbor: University of Michigan Press.

Fortanet, I. (2008). Evaluative language in peer review referee reports. *Journal of English for Academic Purposes, 7*, 27–37.

Giltrow, J. (2005). *Academic writing: An introduction*. Peterborough, ON: Broadview Press.

Gosden, H. (1992). Research writing and NSSs: From the editors. *Journal of Second Language Writing, 1*, 123–139.

Gosden, H. (2003). "Why not give us the full story?": Functions of referees' comments in peer reviews of scientific papers. *Journal of English for Academic Purposes, 2*, 87–101.

Griffin, K. (September/October 2005). You're wiser now. *AARP: The Magazine*, 51–52.

Halliday, M. A. K. (1989). *Spoken and written language*. Oxford, U.K.: Oxford University Press.

Hartley, J., & Betts, L. (2009). Publishing before the thesis: 58 postgraduate views. *Higher Education Review, 41*(3), 29–44.

Hirano, E. (2009). Research article introductions in English for specific purposes: A comparison between Brazilian Portuguese and English. *English for Specific Purposes, 28*, 240–250.

Hyland, K. (2015). *Academic publishing: Issues and challenges in the construction of knowledge*. Oxford, U.K.: Oxford University Press.

IEEE. (2015). Professional Communication, IEEE Transactions on. Available at: http://ieeexplore.ieee.org.ezproxy1.library.usyd.edu.au/xpl/aboutJournal.jsp?punumber=47

International Committee of Medical Journal Editors. (2009). Uniform Requirements for Manuscripts Submitted to Biomedical Journals: Ethical Considerations in the Conduct and Reporting of Research: Peer Review. Available at http://www.icmje.org/ethical_3peer.html

Jogthong, C. (2001). *Research article introductions in Thai: Genre analysis of academic writing*. (Unpublished doctoral dissertation.) West Virginia University, Morgantown.

Johns, A.M. (1990). L1 composition theories: Implications for developing theories of L2 composition. In B. Kroll. (Ed.), *Second language writing: Research insights for the classroom* (pp. 24–36). Cambridge, U.K.: Cambridge University Press.

Johnson, N.F. (2011). *Publishing from your PhD: Negotiating a crowded jungle*. Farnham, U.K.: Gower.

Kitchin, R., & Fuller, D. (2005). *The academic's guide to publishing*. London: Sage.

Kubota, R. (2003). Striving for original voice in publication? A critical reflection. In C. P. Casanave & S. Vandrick (Eds.), *Writing for scholarly publication: Behind the scenes in language education* (pp. 61–69). Mahwah, NJ: Lawrence Erlbaum.

Kwan, B. (2010). An investigation of instruction in research publishing offered in doctoral programs: The Hong Kong case. *Higher Education, 38*, 207–225.

Lave, J., & Wenger, E. (1991). *Situated learning: Legitimate peripheral participation*. Cambridge, U.K.: University of Cambridge Press.

Lewin, B. A. (2010). *Writing readable research: A guide for students of social science*. London: Equinox.

Li, G. (2012). Getting published and doing research. In R. Kubota & Y. Sun (Eds.), *Demystifying career paths after graduate school* (pp. 151–162). Charlotte, NC: Information Age Publishing.

Li, Y. (2006). A doctoral student of physics writing for publication: A sociopolitically-oriented case study. *English for Specific Purposes, 25*, 456–478.

Lillis, T. M., & Curry, M. J. (2010). *Academic writing in a global context: The politics and practices of publishing in English.* London: Routledge.

Lin, L., & Evans, S. (2012). Structural patterns in empirical research articles: A cross-disciplinary study. *English for Specific Purposes, 31*, 150–160.

Martín, P., & Léon Pérez, I. K. (2014). Convincing peers of the value of one's research: A genre analysis of rhetorical promotion in academic texts. *English for Specific Purposes, 34*(1), 1–13.

McPeek, M. A., DeAngelis, D. L., Shaw, R. G., Moore, A. J., Rausher, M. D., Strong, D. R., Ellison, A. M., Barrett, L., Rieseberg, L., Breed, M. D., Sullivan, J., Osenberg, C. W., Holyoak, M., & Elgar, M. A. (2009). The golden rule of reviewing. *The American Naturalist, 173*(5), E155–E158.

Mungra, P., & Webber, P. (2010). Peer review process in medical research publications: Language and content comments. *English for Specific Purposes, 29*, 45–54.

Murray, R. (2013). *Writing for academic journals* (3rd ed.). Maidenhead, U.K.: Open University Press.

Nackoney, C. K., Munn, S. L., & Fernandez, J. (2011). Learning to write: Wisdom from emerging scholars. In T. S. Rocco, T. Hatcher, & Associates (Eds.), *The handbook of scholarly writing and publishing* (pp. 26–43). San Francisco: Jossey-Bass.

Nature. (2006, December). Overview: Nature's peer review trial. Available at http://www.nature.com/nature/peerreview/debate/nature05535.html

Nonmore, A. H. (2011). The process of transforming the dissertation or thesis into publication. In T. S. Rocco, T. Hatcher, & Associates (Eds.), *The handbook of scholarly writing and publishing* (pp. 75–88). San Francisco: Jossey-Bass.

Olsen, C. M., & Green, A. V. (2012). More evidence of harms of sunbed use, particularly for young people. *British Medical Journal.* DOI: http://dx.doi.org/10.1136/bmj.e6101

Ortega, L. (2015). Research synthesis. In B. Paltridge & A. Phakiti (Eds.), *Research methods in applied linguistics* (pp. 225–244). London: Bloomsbury.

Oxford University Press. (2015). Oxford University Press Journals. Available at http://www.oxfordjournals.org/en/our-journals/index.html

Paltridge, B. (1992). EAP placement testing: An integrated approach. *English for Specific Purposes, 11*, 243–268.

Paltridge, B. (2000). Genre knowledge and teaching professional communication. *IEEE Transactions on Professional Communication, 43*(4), 1–4.

Paltridge, B. (2002). Thesis and dissertation writing: An examination of published advice and actual practice. *English for Specific Purposes, 21,* 125–143.

Paltridge, B. (2013). Learning to review submissions to peer reviewed journals: How do they do it? *International Journal for Researcher Development, 4,* 6–18.

Paltridge, B. (2015a). Referees' comments on submissions to peer-reviewed journals: When is a suggestion not a suggestion? *Studies in Higher Education, 40,* 106–122.

Paltridge, B. (2015b). Thesis and dissertation writing: An examination of published advice and actual practice. In H. Basturkman (Ed.), *English for academic purposes. Volume 1.* Abingdon, U.K.: Routledge.

Paltridge, B., & Mahboob, A. (2014a). In this issue. *TESOL Quarterly, 48,* 651–654.

Paltridge, B., & Mahboob, A. (2014b). In this issue. *TESOL Quarterly, 48,* 1–5.

Paltridge, B., & Mahboob, A. (2015). In this issue. *TESOL Quarterly, 49,* 1–5.

Paltridge, B., Starfield, S., Ravelli, L., & Tuckwell, K. (2012). Change and stability: Examining the marcostructures of doctoral theses in the visual and performing arts. *Journal of English for Academic Purposes, 11,* 332–334.

Paltridge, B., Starfield, S., & Tardy, C. M. (2016). *Ethnographic perspectives on academic writing.* Oxford, U.K.: Oxford University Press.

Prater, C. (2014). 8 ways to identify a questionable open access journal. *American Journal Experts.* Available at: https://www.aje.com/en/author-resources/articles/8-ways-identify-questionable-open-access-journal

Quirk, R., Greenbaum, S., Leech, G., & Svartvik, J. (1985*). A comprehensive grammar of the English language.* Harlow, U.K.: Longman.

Rocco, T. S. (2011). Reasons to write, writing opportunities, and other considerations. In T. S. Rocco, T. Hatcher, & Associates (Eds.), *The handbook of scholarly writing and publishing* (pp. 3–12). San Francisco: Jossey-Bass.

Rozycki, W., & Johnson, N. (2013). Non-canonical grammar in best paper award winners in engineering. *English for Specific Purposes, 32,* 157–169.

Sage. (2015). Journals. http://www.sagepub.com/journals.nav

Springer. (n.d.). Springer's journal collections. Available at https://www.springer.com/gp/eproducts/springer-journals

Swales, J. M. (1990). *Genre analysis: English in academic and research settings.* Cambridge, U.K.: Cambridge University Press.

Swales, J. M. (2004). *Research genres: Explorations and applications.* New York: Cambridge University Press.

Swales, J. M., & Feak, C. B. (2009). *Abstracts and the writing of abstracts.* Ann Arbor: University of Michigan Press.

Swales, J. M., & Feak, C. B. (2012). *Academic writing for graduate students: Essential tasks and skills* (3rd ed.). Ann Arbor: University of Michigan Press.

Taylor & Francis. (2015). Journals at Taylor & Francis Onine. Available at http://www.tandf.co.uk/journals/

Thomson, P. (2011). How to give feedback on a peer's paper. Available at patthomson.wordpress.com/2011/07/18/how-to-give-feedback-on-a-peers-paper/

Thomson, P., & Kamler, B. (2013). *Writing for peer reviewed journals: Strategies for getting published.* Abingdon, U.K.: Routledge.

University of California Press. (2015). Journals on UCPRESSJOURNALS.COM. Available at http://www.ucpress.edu/ucpjournals.php

University of Chicago Press. (n.d.). University of Chicago Press Journals. Available at http://www.press.uchicago.edu/journals.html

Universiteit van Amsterdam. (2010). *Doctorate regulations of the University of Amsterdam 2010.* Amsterdam: Doctorate Board, Universiteit van Amsterdam.

Wager E., & Kleinert S. (2011). Responsible research publication: International standards for authors. A position statement developed at the Second World Conference on Research Integrity, Singapore, July 22–24, 2010. In T. Mayer & N. Steneck (Eds.), *Promoting research integrity in a global environment* (pp. 309–316). Singapore: Imperial College Press/World Scientific Publishing. Available at http://publicationethics.org/files/International%20standards_authors_for%20website_11_Nov_2011.pdf

Ware, M., & Mabe, M. (2012). *The STM report: An overview of scientific and scholarly journal publishing* (3rd ed.). Oxford, U.K.: International Association of Scientific, Technical and Medical Publishers.

Wellington, J., & Torgerson, C. J. (2005). Writing for publication: What counts as a 'high status, eminent academic journal'? *Journal of Further and Higher Education, 29,* 35–48.

Wiley. (2015). Wiley Online Library. Available at: au.wiley.com/WileyCDA/Brand/id-29.html?&category=For+Working

Zuengler, J., & Carroll, H. (2010). Reflections on the steady increase in submissions. *The Modern Language Journal, 94,* 637–638.